Archery

The #1 Beginner's Guide for Everything An Archer Needs to Know About Recurve And Compound Bows

ALBERT DAWSON

Copyright 2019 © Albert Dawson
All rights reserved.

No part of this guide may be reproduced in any form without permission in writing from the publisher except in the case of review.

Legal & Disclaimer

The following document is reproduced below with the goal of providing information that is as accurate and reliable as possible.

This declaration is deemed fair and valid by both the American Bar Association and the Committee of Publishers Association and is legally binding throughout the United States.

Furthermore, the transmission, duplication or reproduction of any of the following work including specific information will be considered an illegal act irrespective of if it is done electronically or in print. This extends to creating a secondary or tertiary copy of the work or a recorded copy and is only allowed with an express written consent from the Publisher. All additional right reserved.

The information in the following pages is broadly considered to be a truthful and accurate account of facts, and as such any inattention, use or misuse of the information in question by the reader will render any resulting actions solely under their purview. There are no scenarios in which the publisher or the original author of this work can be in any fashion deemed liable for any hardship or damages that may befall them after undertaking information described herein.

Additionally, the information in the following pages is intended only for informational purposes and should thus be thought of as universal. As befitting its nature, it is presented without assurance regarding its prolonged validity or interim quality. Trademarks that are mentioned are done without written consent and can in no way be considered an endorsement from the trademark holder.

Table of Contents

Introduction 11
Chapter 1: A brief history of Archery 19
    Archery in mythology 27
    Archery as a sport 30
    Archery in hunting... 35
    Archery's place is modern society 37
Chapter 2: Equipment and accessories used in archery 42
    Types of bows... 46
    The recurve bow 54
    The compound bow 58
    Types of arrows... 64
    Accessories used in archery.......................... 76
    How to choose the right products and brands 78
Chapter 3: Beginning to shoot 81
    General guidelines for archers 88
    Fundamentals of shooting............................ 93
    Basic safety precautions 103

Physical fitness 107
Mental preparation 109
Chapter 4: Common mistakes and how to avoid them 112
Mistake number one: not backing down from a shot 113
Mistake number two: focusing too much on aiming 115
Mistake number three: not following through 117
Mistake number four: improper release 119
Mistake number five: dwelling on the misses 120
Mistake number six: fixing what isn't broken 122
Mistake number seven: cluttered mind 124
Mistake number eight: Incorrect draw length 125
Mistake number nine: punching it 127
Mistake number one: losing your target 129
Mistake number two: forcing your aim 131

Mistake number three: holding on too long 132
Mistake number four: going against the wind 133
Mistake number five: worrying too much on equipment 135
Mistake number six: losing form................ 136
Mistake number seven: you forget to push... 138
Mistake number eight: panic! 139
Mistake number nine: trying to be perfect 141

Chapter 6: Becoming a successful archer 144
Factor number one: nutrition and conditioning...147
Factor number two: mental concentration and focus 152
Factor number three: practice.................... 158
Factor number four: tracking performance..165
One final thought... 169

Chapter 5: Becoming a successful archer 172

Factor number one: nutrition and conditioning 175
Factor number two: mental concentration and focus 180
Factor number three: practice 186
Factor number four: tracking performance 193
One final thought... 197
Chapter 6: Tournament competition 200
Main guidelines for tournament competition 202
Target Archery 202
Types of bows used in target archery tournaments 203
Target archery tournament format 206
Mind the whistle 211
Length of target archery tournaments 213
Target archery tournament scoring 214
Field archery tournaments 215
Bows used in field archery 218
Field archery individual tournaments 219
Field archery team tournaments 221

NFAA Field Tournaments 223
3D Archery Tournaments 224
Tips and strategies for tournament competition 225
Equipment and accessories used in tournament competition 229

Chapter 7: About equipment upgrades and maintenance 233
General guidelines about equipment maintenance 234
The importance of having finely tuned equipment 235
Make a quick inspection of your equipment after every shot 237
Ensure that you riser is safe to use 237
Taking care of the bow string 240
Store your bow properly 244
Have an annual inspection done by a recognized expert 246
Avoid dry firing at all costs 247
How to know if upgrades are needed 254

Cost considerations 256
Conclusion 260

Introduction

Thank you for purchasing, "Archery: The #1 Beginner's Guide for Everything An Archer Needs to Know About Recurve And Compound Bows". If you have picked up this volume it is because you are serious about getting started in the world of archery. In the mainstream, most people believe archery to be some part of an archaic style of warfare that is limited to films such as "Lord of the Rings".

However, that could not be farther from the truth.

Archery is very much alive and kicking today. Granted, it has become a bit of a niche sport. Nevertheless, it maintains a good deal of popularity among athletes, both amateur and Olympic, as well as outdoorsmen and hunters.

Definitely, archery enthusiasts and aficionados are very much inclined to pursuing all things related to this sport. As a matter of fact, it is one of the few sports which can translate into a practical application in the real world such as the case of hunting.

So, whether you are an aspiring hunter or just a concerned parent looking for an interesting sport for their child, archery has an appeal to everyone. Archery is also popular among historians, especially military historians as it holds a very interesting appeal throughout history.

That is why this book, which is written as a guide, is meant to take the novice archer and transform them into a serviceable archer. Again, the ultimate goal of your interest in archery will greatly depend is you are into sports or hunting. Nevertheless, the fundamentals are the same.

We will also discuss the basic techniques used in archery, that is, the fundamentals of actual shooting. As such, we will be looking at how you can pick up your first bow and arrow and make your first successful shot.

Also, we will be looking at what equipment you should be considering, especially as a novice, and what type of equipment would make sense initially. Furthermore, we will discuss some of the basics with regard to equipment maintenance and even upgrades.

In addition, we will be taking a look at some aspect which you may not have thought of such as conditioning and nutrition. Additionally, we will take a look at the proper mindset needed by a successful archer.

As you can see, this guide, although somewhat brief, contains all of the information you will need in order to get started in a single volume. Of course, there are many other books and guides out there. Yet, they don't include as many details in a compact and concise manner. Given the pace of modern life, being straightforward is certainly an important quality to have.

As such, this guide is intended to walk you through the process of getting started with your newfound passion, hobby or discipline. In fact, archery is so widespread that there are entire cultural organizations built around it.

For instance, you may find folks who engage in medieval reenactments. In addition, renaissance fairs often pit archers in a duel using rudimentary bows and arrows just the ones that were used back in the middle ages.

These competitions are often entertaining and filled with wonderful opportunities for social interaction and participation. Winners generally attain status as legendary archers as they compete on equal footing with their counterparts from hundreds of years ago.

For more modern athletes, modern archery equipment has been designed to improve distance and accuracy. Moreover, modern archery draws on much of the parameters found in competitions with firearms. Though the equipment is different, the concept behind each type of competition largely remains the same.

In the case of outdoorsmen and hunters, archery offers a huge advantage in terms of stealth and effectiveness as compared to the use of firearms. Since prey are easily scared in the woods, the use of bows and arrows allows hunters to sneak up on their prey without causing too much noise.

The use or archery also offers a more "natural" experience in that the lack of firearms resembles the hunting techniques that would have been used by hunters thousands of years ago. This is an appealing trait to some outdoorsmen who are looking to capture the feeling that comes using this type of weapon.

So, what are you waiting for?

Let's take a closer look at what this guide can do for you in getting your started with your newfound interest. The information contained herein will surely make it easy for you to get your feet wet. But most importantly, you will be able to make an informed decision about what you need before actually going out there and purchasing a bunch of equipment.

If after reading this guide you realize that archery may not be the right sport for you, then fear not. That is also perfectly fine. Indeed, archery isn't for everyone. But if you do feel that this is something which you can find value in, then you will not be disappointed. This is the type of sport that will grow on you. Much like golf, it is the type of sport that can make for hours of relaxation and concentration.

So, if you are looking for a sport which can appeal young and old, but especially for older children and teenagers, then you have come to the right place. If this is something in which you have always been interested in, then you will surely find a great deal of opportunity for fun.

Ultimately, your choice of this sport will lead you down a lifestyle that will surely have you focused and committed on improving your technique. Again, archery is like golf in that you need to master your technique before you can move from begin "good" to being "exceptional". The best thing about archery is that there are no special abilities needed. All you need is the willingness and the desire to try your best.

As you gain proficiency and skill at this sport, you will find it to be exceptionally rewarding and satisfying. This is the type of sport that requires dedication to excel at. That is why you will feel very proud of yourself, or your loved ones, when you are able to achieve success.

Chapter 1: A brief history of Archery

Archery is one of the oldest activities known by humans in recorded history.

As a matter of fact, there are cave paintings that remote back to 20,000 BC in which the use of a bow and arrow is illustrated in hunting activities.

Indeed, the use of the bow and arrow is about as old as human civilization. While it is unclear at which point it use made its way onto the scene, it is clear that the use of the bow and arrow was a clear innovation for what were still largely hunter-gatherer civilizations.

The use of the bow and arrow in warfare is also the subject of much speculation. It is believed that as soon as humans discovered its use for hunting purposes, the next step what its use in fighting. For instance, the Nubian cultures around Egypt way back around 10,000 BC are some of the first peoples known to have used the bow and arrow for the purpose of hunting and fighting.

If you really think about it in terms of ancient civilizations, this was a considerable innovation comparable to the automatic rifle first used in the late nineteenth century. The rate of fire provided by archers in ancient warfare was about as impressive as a Gatlin gun was back in the Old West.

Without delving too much into ancient warfare and fighting techniques, it is safe to say that the use of bow and arrows in warfare proved to be the main catalyst for its improvement and evolution over time. This is why we will be taking a look at some of the innovations brought about by war in order to gain a better understanding of how the bow and arrow came to be what they are today.

Some of the evolutions on the regular bow and arrow such as the crossbow, the ballista and catapult, which all rely on some type of drawstring or slingshot action, were also logic consequences to the progress made by human civilization. These were mainly warfighting creations. For the sake of this volume, we will stick to the use of bows and arrows in sport and hunting. While the use of the bow and arrow in warfare is certainly a fascinating topic, it shall remain a topic for a future volume.

Consequently, the traditional bow and arrow as used by hunters did not evolve much for hundreds, if not, thousands of years. Some logical upgrades we made insofar as the type of wood used for the bow itself, the type of materials used for the arrow bodies in addition to the materials used for the arrowheads.

Archeological digs throughout the world have revealed the use of stone and animal bone in early arrowheads, while more sophisticated materials used by ancient cultures include jade and obsidian as seen in Maya and Aztec sites. The Native American tribes of North America also used stones and animal bones to develop their early arrowheads though the use of stone seemed to have been preferred over animal bone.

The use of metal in arrowheads was not seen until the develop of metallurgy in Europe. The discovery and use of metals, around the time of the Stone Age, ushered in a new type of innovation and invention.

The first metals to be discovered by prehistoric humans were gold, silver and copper. Around

9,000 BC Earth mineral were so abundant that they lay on the surface. It was common to have animals dig up gold nuggets or even chunks of copper. Over the next several hundreds of years, humans learned that metals could be used for different purposes.

While there are indications as to the use of gold in early arrowheads, the understanding of gold as a valuable commodity quickly ended its use in other forms that wasn't jewelry (as seen in prehistoric emperors) or a monetary metal.

So, it wasn't until iron was discovered that humans realized that it could be used to replace stone and animal bone in the creation of tools and weapons. The Iron Age brought about the develop of weapons such as swords while the develop of iron arrowheads provided superior quality and strength to the previous arrowheads made of obsidian.

In addition, iron was far more malleable than stone. Consequently, it could be easily shaped into any way that was seen fit. Furthermore, metals tended to last a lot longer than animal bone though they weren't quite as resistant as obsidian.

However, the main reason for replacing stone arrowheads with metal ones was due to the fact that metals were a lot more abundant that stones like obsidian and jade. This made it a lot easier for craftsmen to find them and be able to keep with production demands.

Ancient civilizations that used archery for both hunting and warfare include the Chinese of the Shang Dyntasy around 1,700 BC and the Japanese as late as the sixth century BC. The Japanese, in particular, used a longbow that measure over 2 meters. This is particularly striking as the use of the longbow didn't become popular in Europe until the middle ages. The medieval legends of Robin Hood and his merry band of thieves evokes recollections of the longbow.

Eventually, the use of the bow and arrow came to a crescendo in ancient Greece. The Greeks were known to have perfected the art of archery in the Old World. Although there were other warrior civilizations such as the Spartans who were based more on hand to hand combat, the Greeks were very much adept at using archery in all walks of life.

The ancient Egyptians and Persians also used archery for war fighting and hunting applications. The Turks were also one of the most prolific civilizations to use the bow and arrow in all capacities. However, it was during the middle ages that the bow and arrow truly achieved their height as its use, in addition to the crossbow, were the subject of much legend and folklore.

Since the advent of gunpowder and consequently firearms, the bow and arrow began losing appeal in the combat as well as hunting. Since the rifles began replacing arrows, these began falling more into the category of sport and hunting.

While some depictions of the use of bows by special forces during the Vietnam War persist to this day, its use has largely fallen out of favor by military practitioners. The Hollywood film franchise "Rambo" immortalized the actor Sylvester Stallone using arrows with explosive-tipped arrowheads to shoot down aircraft.

To this day, archery is thriving though in a much different application and capacity.

Archery in mythology

The popularity and appeal of archery is literally inundated throughout mythology and folklore. The most common stories that persist to this day are those of the Middle Ages in which Robin Hood, the legendary longbowman famously split the arrow of another competitor in half. Robin Hood has been immortalized in tales, ballads and most notably, in Hollywood films.

Of course, Robin Hood was not the only archer during the Middle Ages. In fact, archers were considered one of the most important soldiers in all medieval armies. They had the purpose of allowing foot soldiers to gain ground on their opponents. This is why the allure of being a skilled archer allowed for the creation of many different folk tales and legends.

Another example of archers in mythology is Odysseus. Odysseus, who appears in the famous work, The Odyssey, written by Homer, depicts Odysseus as being particularly skilled at archery. The work goes on to describe how Odysseus's wife, Penelope, after a 20-year absence by Odysseus, resolves to take on another husband.

She challenges all of her potential suitors to draw her husband's bow and shoot in order to prove their worth. Odysseus, who had returned alive from the Trojan War, is disguised as a shepherd. In order to prove to his wife who he really is, he is able to draw his own bow and prove who he really was.

While this tale is believed to be largely a work of fiction, it is highly representative of the power and attracting that archery has in the world of mythology. Thus, archery has always been considered as having a higher status as compared to other types of trades in war fighting and society. After all, how many legends were built around wielding a battering ram?

Another epic episode comes from the Spartans and their war against the Persians. This tale comes from the Battle of the Thermopylae in which King Leonidas and his 300 intended to stop the Persian army, led by Xerxes, from advancing.

During this battle, Xerxes ordered his archers to fire upon 5,000 arrows at the Spartan resistance. This barrage of arrows was enough to weaken their position but not eliminate the Spartan stronghold. In the end, Leonidas and his 300 were overrun by some 10,000 Persians. Yet, the heroic tale is punctuated by the power and might of the Persian bowmen.

Archery is also the subject of many fantasy tales revolving around medieval themes. While these tales range from books to major Hollywood motion pictures, the main characters tend to involve the use of archery in some capacity. In addition, these tales also tend to involve some type of magical component to the characters.

Indeed, mythology has been a breeding ground for archery. Additionally, Hollywood has done its fair share to keep the spirit or archery alive. Thus, it is not unheard of for someone to have a genuine interest in archery, both from a historical perspective, as well as, a practical one.

Archery as a sport

Since archery has largely fallen out of use in terms of military applications, it has largely been relegated as a sport. Save for outdoorsmen and survivalists, archery is mainly seen as a sport in the modern world.

This has led to vast improvements in both technique and equipment. Moreover, there has been a lot more regulation of archery since its inception as a sport. This is key as archery is an Olympic sport. Therefore, it must have the checks and balances that all Olympic sports must have, both in terms of qualifying and in terms of the actual competition itself.

Archery debuted in 1900 at the Games of the II Olympiad in Paris. It would stay on the books until 1920 while missing the 1912 games. Archery was dropped after the 1920 games. In this first era of Olympic archery, Belgium won 11 gold medals taking a total of 20. The governing body for this initial event was the World Archery Federation.

After its hiatus, archery returned to the Olympics at the 1972 Munich Games. Since then, the sport has been contested with South Korean archers being the predominant force in this sport. Since 1972, South Koreans have taken a total of 23 gold medals. The United States holds second place with 8 gold medals since 1972. Given the fact that archery has been on the books as an Olympic sport since 1972, it has gained popularity and acceptance.

The World Archery Federation (WAF) holds several events and tournaments at various times in order to earn points for Olympic qualifying. There are approximately 156 federated nations. Given that this is the official governing body for the sport, the Olympic standards mirror those of the WAF. This provides structure and standardization to the sport all over the world.

Since 2006, the World Cup of Archery is held. This event looks to gather the best archers from all over the world in a format that consists of four rounds which are completed throughout the year. As such, it is not a single event held at a specific time of year, but rather, it is a series of events that lead to the eventual champion both in individual categories, as well as, team categories.

There is also an Indoor World Cup that is played during winter months. It was inaugurated for the 2010-2011 season. It consists of three rounds as opposed to four.

The current top-ranked male and female archers in the recurve category are from South Korea. The top-ranked male compound leader is from the Netherlands while the top-ranked female archer is from Turkey.

The world rankings are published following major events and may be subject to change after each event. Rankings are determined by a points system in which such points are accumulated after placements following each event.

The two main championships reflect the two main types of bows used in modern archery: the recurve and the compound. Each category has an individual men's and women's competition. It also holds and men's and women's team competition with an additional mixed teams competition.

As you can see, archery holds significant following as a sport. It not only counts with internationally sanctioned events but has held its place firmly at the Olympics. Since the Olympics are notorious for dropping unpopular sports, such as the case of baseball and softball, the fact that archery has maintained its status is a testament to the overall acceptance of it as a sport.

Archery in hunting

As described earlier, the other major application of archery in modern society is hunting. There are various laws governing the use of bows in hunting (including crossbows), it is worth to consult with your local authorities on the laws governing this practice.

In general, the use of bows is subject to the same legislation that governs the use of firearms for hunting purposes. Some countries and individual states list bows (specially crossbows) as dangerous weapons. So, holding a compound bow in some countries may be just as bad a being caught with an AK-47 in the trunk of your car. There are also hunting licenses which you may have to procure in order to hunt freely.

Other countries have outlawed hunting altogether as they have had issues with illegal poaching. Needless to say, this is more a matter of wildlife conservation that the consideration of a bow as a lethal weapon.

In addition, some countries and individual states regulate the sale of bows and their accessories under the same guidelines as firearms. Thus, anyone who purchases a bow, or a crossbow, would have to go through the same background check process as they would is the event of purchasing a handgun.

Beyond that, it is perfectly fine to carry a bow so long as it is not used in any criminal activity. Bows are perfectly fine for recreational purposes though you may find some security concerns from airport officials should you choose to travel with one.

Archery's place is modern society

Archery is still very much alive and kicking. It does not seem like it is going to be fading away any time soon. As such, its popularity is only increasing with time. As its following grows more and more, the magnitude of each event and championship will showcase some of the most talented individuals in the world.

A cursory look at the WAF world rankings will reveal that it is truly an international sport. While there may be some predominance from South Korea at the moment, archery has a following in Europe, America, Asia and Africa.

Consequently, there is consistent work done on improving equipment and technique by the major players in the archery world. While the fundamentals or archery have remained unchanged for thousands of years, modern technology has allowed for the develop of better materials and improved technique.

Of course, purists and historians enjoy giving old-school bows a good workout, but these individuals remain largely enthusiasts. They are generally limited to the renaissance movement. Some will go as far as recreated epic battles though mainly for historical and entertainment purposes. Yet, they have been adept at keeping the spirit of medieval archery alive and well.

As far as for the future of archery, it is an evolving sport. Considering that archery is just like any major sport in that rule changes don't commonly happen, it is hardly a sport which is stuck in the past. Other sports which mirror its long-standing heritage, like golf and tennis, there is a mix of tradition and modernization.

So, the speculation about what the future might

bring is still very much up in the air. Nevertheless, the need for improving upon technique is paramount to gaining an edge at a competitive level. For those hunters, technique is just as important as equipment. That is why a balance needs to be struck between gear and training. No amount of gear can compensate for a lack of training while excellent training can make up for a lack of effective equipment.

For individuals who are serious about taking up archery as a competitive sport, it certainly pays to look at the various options regarding equipment and the price ranges which are available on the market. Making informed decisions about the prices and quality of equipment are paramount to making the ideal choice of equipment.

Later on in this guide, we will be taking a deep look at equipment and what you can hope to acquire as a novice archer. Given the fact that there is a myriad of options available, having information on the various alternatives will go a long way toward acquiring that you will need at the outset of your archery endeavors.

In addition, it is always good to try out various types of equipment at the beginning before settling on a specific type of equipment. To use a metaphor, archery equipment is like running shoes. Most runners will tell you that not all running shoes are the same. They need to try out different pairs of shoes before choosing the right kind for them.

In much the same way, archery equipment is all about finding the right feel for you type of style and competition. You cannot expect to find a one size fits all solution. Hardly. You will find that many of the alternatives out there tailor to the individual needs to the archer. So, do take the time to find the best equipment for you.

Chapter 2: Equipment and accessories used in archery

In this chapter, we are going to be taking a look at the equipment used in archery along with some of the accessories that go along with it.

Archery, as a sport, does require a little bit of hardware. That is why we have devoted an entire chapter to it. As a matter of fact, archery equipment tends to be rather specialized. So, it certainly pays to know and understand what to look for when you are shopping for your gear.

The first word of caution that I would like to give you at this point is to beware of going in headfirst and purchasing all of the equipment you feel you will need up front. Since archery equipment can be a little bit hard to find and can get pricey if you don't shop around, my advice is for you to finish this chapter first before making any purchase decisions.

Of course, you can start to take a look at what type of equipment is available in your location. It might be that you will find some very good options near you. However, if you happen to find that there aren't many options available in your area, you might consider purchasing your gear online.

Naturally, the best way to go would be to actually se it and try it out before you actually make a purchase. One alternative that I always suggest is to approach archery schools and trainers. Since they have all the equipment you need, you can test it out as part of your training lessons or just shooting on the range for fun. That will allow you to get a feel for the various type of equipment available.

For instance, you might try your hand at shooting a recurve bow, that is, the simplest form of the bow; the kind that doesn't have all of the various sights and balances. Or, you can the compound bow which is far more sophisticated and offers the greatest amount of range of accuracy.

By trying out both of these types of bows, you can get a feel for which one you would like to begin training on. Most archers generally try their hand at both types of bow before choosing one to specialize in. In fact, if you choose to sign up to an archery range and/or take classes, you can rent out their equipment before making up your mind on which equipment you might consider buying eventually.

There is also one other consideration: while we all hope that you make archery a lifelong passion, sometimes it just doesn't work out.

There are folks who give archery a try only to realize it wasn't meant to be something they would enjoy for years to come. Yet, they end up getting stuck with costly equipment they may not use ever again.

In a way, it is like spending a bunch of money on golf clubs, tennis rackets or a mountain bike which will only gather dust in the garage. That is why it is highly recommended that you give archery an initial go around on rented equipment while you truly find your bearings.

Then, once you decide if you would like to try the recurve or compound bow, you can be sure that you have made a choice following your heart and your passion. At the end of the day, archery is meant to be a mentally challenging sport while having requisite physical demand from athletes.

Types of bows

The first and foremost element of archery is the bow. This is on the most iconic pieces of military hardware, folklore and culture that the world has come to know. Virtually all cultures of the world have some sort of tradition indicating the use of the bow and arrow.

Given the fact that virtually every culture throughout the world came to use the bow and arrow in hunting and fighting, it is safe to say that this is the type of invention that is a logical consequence of human intelligence. One other such invention can be seen in the wheel. Virtually all of the cultures in human civilization figured out that using the wheel made work a lot easier.

Consequently, the evolution of the bow has undergone several transformations over the thousands of years in which it has existed.

Initially, the first bows were made of curved animal bones, such as ribs of large mammals. The drawstrings were produced from several types of natural fibers most notably hemp. Over time, the need for a more flexible type of material was needed. In addition, making bows of out lighter material made it easier to carry them around. Since bows were invented for hunting, early hunters needed to have a more portable device which would allow them to cover longer distances in search of prey.

As bow construction evolved, the transition to wood was a logical consequence. Several types of wood have been used over the centuries in bow construction. The most popular type of wood used in bow construction is maple. While virtually any type of wood can be used to construct bows, the main drawback with stiffer wood is its lack of flexibility.

As such, wooden bows need a firm, yet flexible wood that won't break under the tensile strength of pulling back on the drawstring, also known as a bowstring. Stronger types of wood are used on crossbows and ballistas since these have much higher rates of tensile strength and do not require nearly as much flexibility as a traditional handheld bow.

At first, bows were made of a single type of wood with a rough finish. Throughout the middle ages, it was believed that the varnish or lacquer used to seal the bow's finish influenced a great deal of the bow's performance. This is largely a myth as it has been proven that the type of wood itself plays a far greater role in determining the bows performance as opposed to any finishing the bow might have.

The emergences of the composite bow created a much more flexible and agile bow due to its improved strength, flexibility is resistance. In essence, a composite bow consisted of having the contain several layers of material piled on top of it. It was common to incorporate strong animal bones in the center and ends of the bow while adding wooden layers covering the core of the bow. This allow for increased tensile strength and thereby greater range.

Of course, traditional bow lacked any type of sighting capabilities. The left archers to mainly rely on their instincts and judgment. Without any type of guidance, archery was mainly an art and often meant missing targets at longer distances. This is why crossbows were considered to have been far more effective than traditional bows as they offered similar ranges and improved accuracy.

The emergence of the longbow was a game changer in medieval warfare. The longbow typically measured over two meters in length. It offered improved accuracy and range than any other type of traditional bow. The recurve bow is the modern version of the traditional medieval longbow.

Figure 1. An artist's rendering of a traditional longbowman.

As you can see in Figure 1, traditional longbowmen relied on their vision and instincts for targeting purposes. They typical carried a short sword in case of hand to hand combat. Arrows could be carried similarly to a backpack slung across their backs or around their waist.

There was no specific place for quivers to be carried though it largely relied on the archer's particular preference.

The invention of the thumb ring the in the later years of the middle ages and the renaissance introduced the first targeting mechanisms that archers could use in order to hit targets more accurately. Similar types of rings were added to the bows themselves in the latter stages of the renaissance. However, improvements upon the longbow fell to the wayside with the rise of firearms. The first working versions of rifles and shotguns stunted any further development of the longbow.

Since archery was relegated to the domain of sport, further improvements upon the traditional bow led to the development or improved sighting and targeting mechanisms. While the traditional longbow is alive and well, very little has changed about it since the renaissance.

Further improvements on bows led to the development of the compound bow. This is the most commonly known type of bow today. It has hunting and warfighting applications. In military terms, the compound bow was famously used by United States special forces in Vietnam. As mentioned earlier, this is the type of bow used by actor Sylvester Stallone in the "Rambo" Hollywood franchise.

The bow is still used by several military special forces throughout the world since it is the most silent type of weapon available today. It is ideal for concealment and stealth. Since it is silent, it is a weapon of choice for jungle warfare. The longbow and short sword of a medieval soldier are now replaced by a compound bow and a machete.

To this day, United States special forces have immortalized the role of the bow in their insignia by wearing crests featuring to interlocked arrows.

The recurve bow

The recurve bow is the modern-day successor of the longbow. It lacks many of the improvements made on the compound bow. Mainly, a recurve bow doesn't lack any of the synthetic materials that are used in compounds bows such as metals, polymer or plastic.

As such, the recurve bow is still made of wood, with several types of wood used, most notable pine (the same type of wood used in hockey sticks and baseball bats). In addition, some manufacturers still use natural fibers as well as animal gut in the production of bow strings.

These types of bows have far less range and accuracy than compound bows.

They are the favorite of purists and enthusiasts who believe that archery should remain as it did back in the middle ages. This is why archery, as an Olympic sport, features this category. In a way it is like comparing apples with apples.

Figure 2. A modern recurve bow with arrows

Figure 2 highlights the nature of a modern recurve bow. It is plain to see that there isn't much difference between this type of bow as compared to traditional longbows that legends such as Robin Hood would have once used.

One of the main differences between the traditional longbow and a recurve bow is that traditional longbows were rounded all around. This included some type of leather covering for the grips. Modern recurve bows tend to have a flat shape all around with rounded sections for the grip. Some types of recurve bows feature a type of hollow pieces that resembles a handle. This provides greater control and allows for greater tensile strength.

Beyond that, the most advanced sighting features on a recurve bow may be the use of thumb rings. Although, most recurve bow archers will forego any type of additional aids and rely solely on their vision and judgment.

Figure 3. Recurve bow grip.

Figure 3 clearly illustrates a traditional recurve bow grip which the hand holding the bow lacks any additional targeting or sighting aids. Some archers opt to use a leather glove in order to relieve the friction that results from the arrow being fired. This is more an issue of comfort than practicality.

A typical recurve bow may have a range of about 100 yards with some of the elite archers in the world being able to surpass that range. Although, any distance greater than 100 yards tends to lose accuracy on a recurve bow. Compound bows can easily surpass that range.

The compound bow

The compound bow is the "evolution" of the traditional longbow. It has improved sighting and targeting features in addition to being lighter and made of materials other than wood. This is the bow mentioned in the "Rambo" films and it is the one which is most commonly used in hunting and military applications.

The compound bow is absolutely deadly at close range. Most hunter aim to shoot their prey from a range of 20 to 40 yards. At this range, the compound bow virtually cannot miss. Most hunters claim they can effectively fire from a range of 50 to 60 yards. This is largely credible depending on the conditions.

In competition, compound bows, in indoor conditions, can fire upwards of 100 yards accurately. Out in the open, there are archers claiming they can fire well over 300 yards. While this has been proven to be possible, it largely depends on factors, most notably wind, and the type of arrows used. Metal-tipped arrows tend to be heavier thus reducing their range. Lighter arrows also tend to have a shorter range due to their lack of size and weight.

As mentioned earlier, compound bows are made of different materials such a metal, polymer and plastic. It is not uncommon to have these bows contain elements of all three. They are rigid an inflexible as compared to the recurve bow.

Figure 4. An athlete firing a recurve bow in competition

Figure 4 shows a stark contrast of a compound bow with the traditional recurve bow. As you can see, it has improved grips and sighting capabilities. In addition, the use of synthetic materials in its drawstring gives it additional range and accuracy. Additional stabilizing capabilities reduce shooter sway particularly in windy outdoor conditions. However, the biggest difference between a traditional recurve bow and the compound bow is the two pulleys located at the end of the bow. There is one pulley at the top and another at the bottom.

This pulley system wasn't introduced until the 1960s. So, considering that archery has been around for thousands of years, this is a very recent innovation. The pulley system allows the draw string to be adjusted to the various draw weights that an archer may need. As such, the pulley system allows the bow to "compound" the strength of the bow and the archer. This will enable them to find the most comfortable position for them. As such, it is a way of making the bow adapt to the archer instead of having the archer adjust to the bow.

The compound bow in the Figure 4 tends to be used more for competition while shorter more mobile types of bows are used in hunting and military applications.

The compound bow is the most commonly used type of bow is across various fields and disciplines. Ultimately, it is your decision as to which type of bow you feel most comfortable with. Most novice archers try both types of bows before settling on one type. Some archers like to dabble in both through they end up choosing to stick with one type over the other.

While there is not particular requirement in order to choose one type of bow over the other, it generally boils down to the individual archer's preference. This implies that some archers prefer the more "natural" feel of the recurve bow over the more sophisticated feel of the compound bow.

For hunters and outdoorsmen, it is almost a given that the compound bow will be the bow of choice. At the end of the day, it all depends on the type of application and use. For most hobbyists, a regular recurve bow seems to be the best fit as it requires little maintenance and costs a lot less to purchase. Recurve bows are also considered hobby items so they may not be subject to the same type of regulations as compound bows and crossbows.

So, if you are looking to dabble in archery mainly as a hobby rather than a competitive sport or hunting, then a recurve bow may be the right fit for you.

Types of arrows

The other element that comprises archery is the arrow.

Arrows are just as vital as bows. Needless to say, without arrows, bows are essentially useless. While bows could be wielded as a defensive weapon, say to defend against attack in hand to hand combat, they bear very little use beyond this application.

In fact, it was quite often to see archers carry short swords, knives and daggers in order to defend themselves against foot soldiers. Since most archers were not the most skilled of swordsmen, they generally fled once they ran out of arrows.

Nevertheless, arrows remain at the core of archery. Their craftsmanship is just as important as that of the bow itself. Thus, having good quality arrows will provide better precision, accuracy and overall effectiveness.

Arrows consist of the following parts:

- The point, or tip, which is located at the end of the arrow. This is the end that is intended to strike the target. The various types of arrowheads in modern archery can range from regular metal tips to deadlier types such as the bullet type.

- The shaft is the long narrow piece that actually flies through the air. While there isn't one specific length, shorter shafts tend to develop greater speed but less distance. Longer shafts develop greater distances but often less speed and blunt force. These are generally wooden but can also be plastic.

- The fletchings are commonly represented as feathers through common materials in modern arrows are made of plastic tabs. These tabs are used to assist in helping the arrow fly through the air and generate air speed. In addition, fletching reduce wind resistances thereby increasing range and accuracy.

- The nock the groove that is found at the back of the arrow right behind the fletchings. Its purpose is to provide the archer with a steady point upon which to rest the arrow on the drawstring. Some purists forego the use of the nock as medieval archers didn't commonly use it. The use of nocked arrows was an innovation in the renaissance and one of the calling cards of longbowmen.

ARCHERY

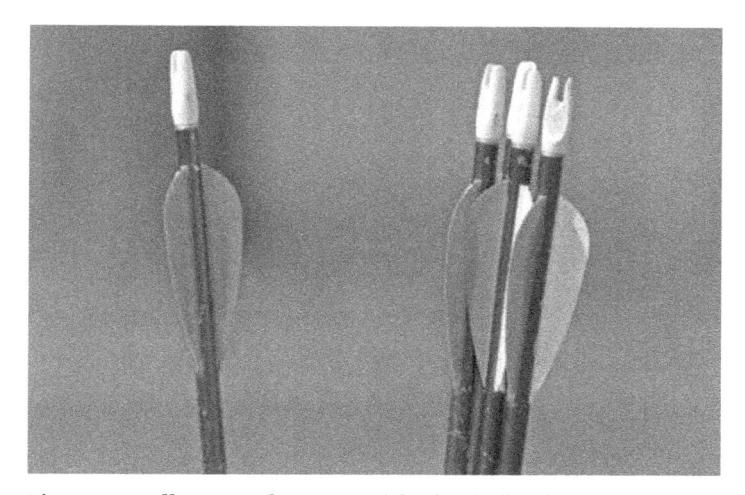

Figure 5. Hollow metal arrows with plastic fletchings and nock.

Figure 5 shows a great depiction of what a modern arrow looks like. If you compare this image to that of arrows depicted in Hollywood films, you can appreciate the significant difference between these and more traditional types of arrows.

The use of hollow metal arrows makes the lighter but also much more resistant upon impact. These allows for the reuse of arrows. Surprisingly, hollow metal arrows such as those made of aluminum, are much lighter than solid wooden arrows. If only medieval archers could have had such upgrades.

The various types of arrowheads or tips depend largely on the type of application. Naturally, hunting applications will require a much more aggressive type of arrowhead whereas competition or hobby use will require standard tips.

Here are some of the most common types of tips or arrowheads.

Bullet. Just as their name suggest, this type of tip is used for accuracy. They are commonly used in competition. The provide a great balance between range and accuracy.

Field or combination. These types of arrowheads taper off at the end creating a thinner tip as compared to a broader based. They are designed for piercing and have both competitive and hunting applications.

Blunt. Blunt points have a flat surface with sharp points. They are not designed quite as much for piercing as they are for killing game in the wild. They are intended to kill prey with blunt force particularly in cranial regions.

Grabbing tips or points. These types of tips resemble grappling hooks. They can be used in combination with rope in order to climb or they are simply used so they can grab onto something and thereby making it easier to locate them. These are, by far, the most expensive type of arrowhead.

Fishing. Fishing tips are just that; fishing tips. They are used to catch fish in shallow waters. They are also used for spear fishing.

Broadheads. These were the standard issue during the middle ages. They were capable of piercing armor and mail. With enough impacts, they could break through metal shields. Some medieval foot soldiers preferred wooden shields as this could catch arrows though it wasn't uncommon to have broadheads bust through wooden shields.

Explosive. These are the arrowheads made famous by Rambo. They contain some type of explosive that will detonate upon impact. The most lethal kinds have nitroglycerine. Others are simply incendiary, that is, will cause a fire upon impact. These have military applications and are not available to the general public.

Figure 6. Artist's rendering of a renaissance longbowman using broadhead arrow tips.

The above rendering shows how broadheads where the predominant force during the middle ages. Although, it wasn't uncommon to see stone arrowheads used during this time. When available, obsidian was also used, though these arrowheads were far more precious than regular metal tips.

There are also various types of shafts used in modern arrows. Let's take a look at the most common ones.

Alloy core. These are the most common type of arrow shafts used by professional archers and Olympians. They are the most expensive but the tradeoff between lightness and stiffness provide an excellent balance. They are generally made of carbon fiber along with base metals such as aluminum.

Solid carbon. These arrows are made of carbon fiber. They are great for general use. They are highly effective for both professionals and hobbyists alike. They are expensive but won't snap or break due to repeated use. They also offer excellent integration with various types of arrowheads.

Aluminum. These are hollow such as those depicted in Figure 5. They are great for beginners and have a medium to low price range. These make great practice arrows though not recommended in competition especially if they have been previously used.

Fiberglass. These are recommended for hobbyists such as those enthusiasts at renaissance fairs. They tend to break a lot more easily. These are not recommended for compound bows as they will most likely shatter upon impact. They are cheap. Thus, they make great learning tools for beginners especially children.

Wood. These are the traditional type of arrow. They can be used by all sorts or archers though they are typically preferred by hobbyists and enthusiasts. While they do tend to break and/or splinter, they generally hold up pretty well. These are not recommended for compound bows.

Additionally, there are also various fletching types.

The biggest difference tends to be three or four fletchings per arrow. Naturally, four fletching are better than three especially when considered speed and range. Shorter range arrows would do best with four fletchings such as those used by hunters. The same goes for longer-range arrows especially those used with compound bows. Arrows used by hobbyists need no more than three.

Plastic. These types of fletchings the most common. They can be used with all kinds of arrows and are a standard in competition. They last a long time and provide the best performance.

Feathered. These types of fletchings are used by traditionalists. They offer great flight capability though they tend to make arrows more expensive. They are not generally used in competition unless they are meant to be used in a decorative fashion as they do not offer any significant upgrade in performance.

Finally, nocks can be included as plastic tips on the back end of the arrow as seen in figure 5. In addition, wooden arrows may simply have a groove craved into the back end of it. Virtually all arrows now come with plastic nocks. These are used in competitive play as well.

Accessories used in archery

The fundamentals or archery bows and arrows. But there is so much more to it than that.

Unless you want to be a purist and essentially have bows and arrows and nothing else, you might be interested in finding out about what types of additional accessories and add-ons you can get for your standard bow and arrow.

In general, here are the main types of accessories you can find.

Sights and scopes. These vary in size and range. You can even get scopes similar to those used on guns with the laser pointer. These certainly make for cool aids especially for hunting. Although, most hunters tend to stay away from anything that might reflect sunlight or generate light in the dark. Nevertheless, they can be fun accessories to play around with in a range.

Stabilizers. These are added weights that can help keep you steady especially in windy, outdoor conditions. A stabilizer can be observed in Figure 4 as the archer is shooting into clear open skies. Since he is looking to get maximum range, it is important for him to be able to get as much stability as possible. In other cases, stabilizers can be added to larger compound bows to get further raw power. This all plays into the ability to generate greater tensile strength.

Grips. These can help gain a better handle on the bow itself. They are pretty straightforward. Most of the time it is a comfort issue on the part of the archer.

Arrow rests. These can be placed on a bow in order to facilitate loading and aiming.

Wrist slings. These are a type of glove and wrist protector aimed at keeping the wrist free of friction from the movement of arrows themselves during loading and firing.

While there is a myriad of accessories that can be added on to a regular compound or recurve bows, the ultimate selection of these should depend on your individual needs and pursuits. Most of these accessories are highly regulated in professional and Olympic archery. As such, they are not used as freely as they are by hunters and aficionados. So, it pays to try different things out in order to find the right ones that fit your individual aims.

How to choose the right products and brands

The aim of this section is not to endorse any products or brands. Rather, it is aimed to serve as a reflection. When you are starting out, it is very hard to know which items you think you will need beyond a bow and a quiver full of arrows.

As a matter of fact, most novice archers begin with a regular bow and wooden arrows before they work their way up to other types of bows such as a compound or crossbow. There is also the potential for trying out different types of arrows and arrowheads. By testing them out, you can make sense of what you would like to do both in terms of becoming competitive and just enjoying a great sport.

At the end of the day, it is a question of finding what works best for you. Naturally, this stems from trying out different things in addition to talking with fellow enthusiasts and athletes. They can give you a better understanding of what you can expect when trying out various techniques and accessories.

Furthermore, your own experimentation with the various types of bows, arrows and accessories will lead you to develop a greater understanding of what you can achieve within the world of archery.

Once again, it all depends on what you aim to achieve. Archery, much like golf and tennis, are the types of sports which can lead to years of enjoyment. Since there isn't a specific competitive nature to it, folks from all walks of life enjoy archery throughout their entire lives. So, it certainly pays to take time and get to know everything the sport has to offer, both in terms of experiences as well as equipment, accessories and techniques.

Chapter 3: Beginning to shoot

In this chapter, we are going to begin with the mechanics of shooting with a bow and arrow. The information which we will be covering will be general in nature given the fact that archery isn't just about picking up a bow and an arrow.

It is recommended that you look into an archery academy or coach who can better assist you in developing your technique and style. The most important thing is that you start out becoming familiar with the mechanics of archery.

As such, this chapter will focus on getting you in the right mindset so that you can get started with your endeavors.

The first step to consider when starting out with archery is your overall level of interest. This is important to keep in mind since given your level of interest, you may choose to immerse yourself in training and practice.

For instance, if you are interested in becoming a renaissance enthusiast you might take things easy at first and ease into your own routine. On the other hand, if you are interested in going all-in and competing, then you might choose to ramp up your training regimen in order for you to develop your skills as much as possible.

Based on that, there are three main categories of archers. You will ultimately find yourself in one of these categories. So, take some go over each category. That way, you can wrap your mind around what type of archery sounds most appealing to you.

Hobbyist. This is the type of archer who may have a profound interest in archery but may not be too deeply involved in practicing archery as such. Here, you will find the weekend warrior, or enthusiast who enjoys archery for the love of the sport. In this category, you will find renaissance fair enthusiasts who partake in medieval archery contests.

Of course, you will also find archers who enjoy trying out compound bows and even crossbows much in the same way firearm aficionados hit firing ranges. For hobbyists, shooting with both recurve and compound bows may be a great way of enjoying the best of both worlds. While hobbyists may not necessarily compete at any point but would certainly take part in events and festivals.

Athletes. These individuals are interested in pursuing archery as a sport, more often than not, with aims at competing at some level. In general, you will find youngsters who are starting out in the world of archery and may be interested in developing their skills up to the highest possible levels. This may include youngsters who would be interested in completing at professional levels.

There are several circuits within the United States though Olympic qualifying poses training and competition requirements just like any other type of Olympic sport. The choice of bow largely depends on what the athlete feels comfortable with. While most archers will learn to shoot with both, they will more than likely specialize in one type of bow. It is rather uncommon for archers to compete in both types of bows, it is not unheard of.

Serious archers will find it challenging to continue improving their skills without disciplined training regimen. This will most likely require the assistance of a dedicated coach who can guide the athlete through the process of achieving higher levels of competition. Ultimately, it is up to athlete to see how far they would like to pursue their competitive endeavors.

Hunters. This category of archers does not have competition in mind though they are rather hardcore in their approach. Hunters are active during hunting season though they tend to practice their skills year-round. They are in tune with the latest developments in technology in order to gain further advantage in their hunting activities.

Hunters are not bound by the rules and regulations of competition though they are subject to gaming laws. This is something which is very important to keep in mind as there might be fines and penalties to be paid for infringing upon current regulations.

In addition, hunters will develop their skills in the outdoors. This makes their particular situation unique as they are out in the open with the elements. Given the fact that outdoor weather conditions are nothing like perfectly controlled indoor conditions proper of competition, hunters need to improve upon their skills under duress.

This type of archery also applies to military applications though these are not quite as common and may only be taught as part of cursory training exercises.

Based on these three main categories of archery, you will find one with which you will feel comfortable. Regardless of whichever one you choose to pursue, the type of equipment, accessories and training that you will need may vary greatly.

This is an important consideration given the fact that hobbyists will require much less equipment and gear than professional athletes. Hunters also require very specific gear depending on the type of game they are hunting and the conditions under which they will hunt. Therefore, this will also place certain requirements in terms of cost.

For hobbyists, renting equipment may be an ideal solution. However, hunters and athletes will need to invest in owning their equipment since the demands of competition and hunting may not be met with rental equipment.

At the end of the day, the journey to becoming a proficient archer begins with the selection of the right equipment. Earlier, we made the point of renting equipment since you may not be entirely sure that archery is the right sport for you. If you are considering involving your children in this sport, you may want to be sure that they are very much interested in pursuing archery before investing a considerable amount of money in gear and equipment.

General guidelines for archers

The following section will look into some general guidelines which virtually all archers can follow when starting out. Please bear in mind that no one is born an expert. As such, achieving such status takes time and dedication.

To begin with, it is worthwhile looking for archery clubs, ranges and/or academies in your area. Depending on your level of interest, you may choose to join one of these clubs in order to hone your skills. If you choose to perfect your skills through classes and training, these clubs can afford you that opportunity.

In addition, it is highly recommended that you seek out such places since becoming part of a broader archery community will help you gain new acquaintances and have the chance to interact with more experienced folks who can guide you on your path through archery.

Finding a niche for yourself within a broader archery community will help you ease into the lifestyle that comes with taking up a sport such as this. In addition, if you are interested in renaissance fairs and the like, you should definitely check out groups and festivals in your area. These types of groups always welcome new members as they are consistently seeking to increase their numbers.

The next situation to consider is whether you see to pursues classes and training or prefer to go at it alone. If you are keen of going out into the woods and practicing on your own, then you might find it to be a very relaxing way to connect with nature.

Now, if you are looking to take a competitive turn, then you might want to seriously consider joining a range and taking some lessons. Perhaps all you need is a push in the right direction. While it is true that there are plenty of tutorials online, you might still want to take a couple of lessons just to see if this is right for you.

Additionally, if you are not keen on purchasing your own equipment up front, then checking out a range will certainly help you get your feet wet without breaking the bank until you are absolutely sure this is something that you would like to pursue further.

On the subject of lessons, it is always best to get your initial indoctrination from a pro. Again, there is nothing that says that you must do this but taking some pointers from a pro will certainly help you develop proper form and technique right away. Please bear in mind that making the most of these initial lessons will set you up for success down the road.

In many ways, this is like taking up tennis or golf. Sure, you can try your best to hit the ball with the racket or club, but unless you are a total natural, you may find some areas in your way which need improving. As such, having the help of a pro can certainly go along way.

Hunters may also benefit from some time at the range. Practicing at a range will allow you to experiment with techniques which you might not be able to otherwise put into practice during real-life hunting situations.

If you are after a more complete approach, you may choose to take a basic, or introductory, course. A course of this nature can help you learn all of the basics and fundamentals you need in order to develop your skills right from the very beginning. Introductory courses are available for all ages and can help individuals develop their skills specifically focusing on the type of archery that they are interested in.

One other general guideline is to stop by archery competitions and events. Often, watching can provide you with tips and strategies which you can "steal" from more experienced archers. In a way, you are scouting to see how others do it either in a competitive nature or during a renaissance fair. Whatever the event, taking the time to watch what others are doing can help you learn a trick or two.

Fundamentals of shooting

Once you have gotten your introduction into the world of archery, you are ready to begin firing your first quiver of arrows. Shooting an arrow isn't as complicated as it seems though developing a high level of proficiency and accuracy does require some training and work. Thus, setting yourself up for success from the beginning is essential in the world of archery.

First of all, you need to decide which bow you are going to try your hand at first. If you choose to try your hand at the recurve bow, then your practice and training will be oriented toward developing your skills in that type of bow.

Later, on you may choose to try your hand at the compound bow before making a final decision regarding what type of bow you would like to dedicate more time to. Nevertheless, you can alternate between either bow. However, if you plan to compete, then making a decision early on as to which type of bow you would like is ideal.

Once you have selected a bow, your next consideration must be choosing a bow with the proper poundage. What this refers to is the tensile strength that the drawstring will have. This depends on the size and build of a person.

For instance, a child may need a bow with a draw weight of around 10 to 20 pounds. A fully-grown man may have a draw weight of 35 pounds, for example. In essence, this has nothing to do with physics but everything with the individual characteristics of the archer. Naturally, you will not ask a child to pull on a string and bow that is suited for a man. Likewise, individuals who are taller or heavier will choose heavier bows.

With draw weight in mind, compound bows can be easily adjusted to a given draw weight. Nevertheless, the actual size of the bow will also depend on the height of the individual or their size in the case of children.

The main reason why draw weight is important is due to the physics which will propel the arrow. If the draw weight is too tight, then you may not only injure yourself, but you won't be able to pull it far back enough to make the arrow reach its maximum speed and distance. If the draw weight is too loose, then the arrow will not receive enough energy to propel it through the air. Thus, the effect will not be quite as desired.

The next step to consider is the draw length. This is the distance that your arms reach out. Firstly, it is the distance which your holding arms reaches out. This is the arm which holds the bow in place. Then, your other arm, your drawing arm, will also reach back as it draws on the bow. The length of your arms will ultimately determine the length of arrows which you need to use in order to optimize your shooting.

For instance, you can spread both of your arms out open. Then, measure your arm span from fingertips to fingertips. The total measurement you get should then be divided by 2.5. In addition, add one to two inches on top of this measurement in order to determine the length of your arrows.

As you can see, the length of the arrow is proportionate to your draw length. This will make your form and mechanics ideal when looking to the develop your ideal form. The selection of the materials that the arrows are made of then becomes rather secondary. You can refer to the guide we presented in the previous chapter for in order to consult the types of materials for your arrows.

One very important consideration is determining your dominant eye. Determining your dominant eye is essential in aiming correctly. A general rule of thumb is that if you are right-handed, your dominant eye will be your right, and vice versa.

While this isn't always the case, you can test your dominant eye by aiming with your bow at a fixed point on a wall or target. If the target does not move, then you have found your dominant eye. However, if you find that it does move, then you might be looking through your non-dominant eye. So, it is always a good idea to test out your eyesight with both eyes before committing to one dominant eye.

If you wear eyeglasses, be sure to wear them when shooting. Hunters generally have custom-made carbon fiber eyeglasses which are ideally suited to the outdoor climates and conditions.

So, it certainly pays to have the right eyeglasses if you feel that you need them.

The next important step is your grip. While the grip you have on the bow with your holding hand is fairly straightforward, the grip which you pull back on the draw string is rather unique. You will pull on the drawstring using your index and little fingers while holding the arrow with your middle and ring fingers. The nock will hold the arrow in place. As you develop your technique, you will gauge the exact moment of release.

Figure 7. Proper grip on drawstring and arrow.

Notice that in Figure 7, the archer is wearing finger guards. These are used to prevent the arrow from slipping due to wet or sweaty fingers. In addition, he is drawing the arrow with his left hand. While it is proper form to raise your hand up to your cheek, it is not proper to actually touch your cheek. If you do so, you will alter the release of the arrow and thereby affect its overall trajectory.

Your elbow should also be shoulder high. It should form a triangular shape with your chest. If you do not maintain your elbow level with your shoulder, then you will push the arrow up or down. Of course, if you are looking to shoot in these directions, then you must alter the positioning of your elbow. But under most circumstances, the idea is to shoot straight. Therefore, your elbow and should must be square as much as possible.

Regarding stance, a good rule of thumb is to stand up straight and keep your feet shoulder width apart. You should have one foot placed behind the other. There is no need to cross your feet as if you were bracing for impact.

A proper archery stance resembles that of a good golf swing. Please keep in mind that you ought to strive to stand as tall as you can while balancing your weight on the soles of your feet rather than on your heels or the balls of your feet.

Figure 8. Proper shooting stance while holding a recurve bow.

Figure 8 demonstrates proper stance while holding a recurve bow. The same stance applies to a compound bow though given the added dimensions and weight of a compound bow, there might be a need for the addition of stabilizers particularly under windy conditions.

In general terms, these are the fundamentals of archery. As such, it is up to you to practice and hone your own style. This will allow you to become comfortable with your chosen bow and the type of archery you are looking to practice. Consequently, your choice of archery practice should help you gain perspective into what you are looking to achieve as a part of your interests.

Furthermore, it is certainly advisable for you to consult with a pro, at least at the very beginning, so that you can get a feel for the proper technique and form. Nevertheless, you can perfectly hone your skills through careful practice on your own. Please bear in mind that becoming proficient on your own takes dedication and attention to detail. So, it certainly pays to invest the time in perfect your overall form and style.

Basic safety precautions

As with any potentially life-threatening activity, safety is of the utmost concern. While archery isn't nearly as dangerous as shooting firearms, an errant arrow can seriously injure someone.

Beyond that, you can certainly take care to protect yourself against potential injury from practicing archery.

In general terms, the most vulnerable areas to protect are your hands and fingers in addition to your eyes.

If you do not wear glasses, then just wearing clear coated glasses like those used on firing ranges can certainly help protect your eyes in case of splinters or any other type of debris. This is especially important if you are using wooden bows and arrows. Because of their material, they could snap at any time and catch you flush in the eye.

Additionally, finger and hand guards are great accessories which you can use to protect your hands. Guards such as the ones seen in Figure 7 can go a long way toward protecting your fingers. Also, there are chest and shoulder protectors which can help you keep your clothes away from the draw string while offering you protection from the snap back of the draw string. In the unlikely event that the string should snap, you are wearing additional protection that can keep you from getting hurt.

Figure 9. A competitor wearing a forearm brace.

In Figure 9, we can observe a competitor wearing a forearm brace. This brace allows for improved stability while offering additional protection to the forearm region from friction and the snap back motion of the draw string.

Ultimately, the use of protection will depend on the degree of precaution you are looking to take. With children, it is of the utmost concern to take all of the recommend safety precautions in order to ensure their wellbeing.

At the range itself, there are general safety measures in order to prevent accidents. For instance, any and all spectators should stand behind the archer in order to avoid being struck by an arrow. Furthermore, it is advisable for all team members to wear bright clothing out in the woods in order to avoid being struck by accident.

Consequently, hunters are encouraged to have some type of uniform signal, even if they are wearing camouflage in order to easily detect one another. This can greatly reduce the incidence of accidents out in the woods.

General safety precautions are always important as no one wants to get injured in any way. That is why going to a range makes a lot of sense much in the same way shooting guns at a proper firing range can virtually eliminate the likelihood on a fatal accident.

Physical fitness

Regarding physical fitness, archers need to maintain the physique and conditioning that any athlete would need to. Since there aren't any specific requirements such as needing to bench press a certain amount of weight or having to run a given distance in a specific amount of time, archers simply need to ensure that they are physically fit to take part in the sport.

Since archery does require practitioners to stand for long periods of time, any impairments to standing for prolonged periods of time may play into the mix. Also, if archers have any shoulder or elbow injuries which may affect their performance, it is recommended that they check with their doctor first.

Additionally, back issues may flare up as archers need to stand straight up for long periods of time. This may cause any back or neck issues to flare up.

In general, though, archers should strive to maintain the physical conditioning that a golfer would need. Naturally, this doesn't mean running a 40-yard sprint in under 10 seconds. Although, it wouldn't hurt if you could.

As for hunters and outdoorsmen, being in top physical condition is important. This is due to the time that is spent outdoors dealing with the elements.

Also, check with your doctor if you are taking any medication that would impair you from properly operating a bow or perhaps cause dizziness, drowsiness or fainting.

Beyond that, the physical requirements or archery are such that virtually anyone at any age, with any type of background can take part in the sport. So, it doesn't matter if you don't look like an NFL running back. The important thing is that you are willing to get out there and try your best.

Mental preparation

Like golf, archery requires a good deal of mental concentration. This means that in order to become successful, archers need to control their thoughts and focus on the target they are looking to hit. This is one of the reasons why archery is popular with folks who are looking to relieve stress and find positive ways of focusing their energy.

Furthermore, breathing plays a key role in hitting the mark. Just like shooting a firearm, archers should pull back on the draw string as they inhale, hold their breath and then release at the moment of exhaling. This will allow the least amount of movement on the part of the archer thereby reducing the likelihood of missing the mark.

If you are dealing with very active children, archery can provide a healthy outlet for their energy. If they can't seem to settle down enough to actually focus and concentrate on the target, having them fire off a few arrows without any particular target is good at helping them let out some energy and then focus.

Some archers have mantras they repeat as they are getting ready to shoot. These mantras are just phrases that they repeat while trying to find the right posture.

In the case of hunters, it can be tough to manage breathing especially if they have been chasing after prey. So, using deep breathing techniques can help get a grip on breathing just enough so that a strong shot can be fired away.

Thus, taking a few moments to practice breathing in between shots, especially in competition, can certainly help alleviate excess energy and allow the archer to remain still while lining up their shots. This can increase the chances of hitting the mark right from the first shot.

Please keep in mind that archery is not a highly intensive sport physically speaking, but it does require a well-rounded individual who can control their thoughts and focus on the task at hand. Consequently, taking the time to get into the right mindset can help you get the most out of this wonderful sport.

Chapter 4: Common mistakes and how to avoid them

In this chapter, we are going to be taking a look at the most common mistakes that novice archers make. These mistakes are usually the result of a lack of experience. Thus, they are certainly worth looking into since avoiding them will help you avoid a great deal of headaches.

As a matter of fact, some folks fall into these traps only to come out disappointed at archery. Of course, when you are not very familiar with the sport, it is easy to feel that the sport itself is at fault for not providing you with the experience that you expected. Indeed, taking the time to go over these pitfalls will help you see the sport for what it is.

Yet, as we have said therefore this guide, archery isn't for everyone. It could be that after some time practicing the sport, or after reading this guide even, you realize that it isn't the sport for you. Of course, that's perfectly fair. It is perfectly fair to decide that archery isn't the right fit for you.

Nevertheless, we are here to look at the ways in which you can get the most out of archery while minimizing the potential you may have for any negative experiences.

That being said, Let's take a look at some of the most common mistakes made while using a compound bow.

Mistake number one: not backing down from a shot

Even expert shooters fall prey to this one. There are shots that are just too hard to make or require extra focus and concentration. Yet, you are determined to make it when you don't have it. Unless you are under intense pressure in competition, it is always best to just take a deep breath and refocus. If you can't line up a shot, then close your eyes, breathe and regroup.

Often, all you need is just to clear your mind and attempt to line up your shot again. This is especially true if you are just practicing or taking part in any type of event that isn't a competition. Please bear in mind that archery is meant to be fun and exciting.

Of course, there are folks who are intense competitors and want to do their best at all times. This can lead to unnecessary pressure. As such, it can lead to an individual feeling that archery is too hard and not worth the stress that it comes with. Even if you are in the midst of a high-level competition, please bear in mind that concentration is of the utmost importance. So, repeating a mantra such as "eye, eye on the rye" can be something simple but effective in keeping your mind's eye focused on the target.

Ultimately, the more you are able to focus on your target, the easier it will be for you to manage your breathing, emotions and the people around you.

Mistake number two: focusing too much on aiming

Yes, there is such a thing as focusing too much on aiming.

This happens when a shooter is obsessed with lining up the perfect shot. There is no such a thing as the "perfect shot". What there is, is the right shot for the right circumstances. If you are able to figure out what the right shot is based on your current situation, then you will have a great chance to make it.

When archers focus too much on making the right shot, what ends up happening is that tension building in the back and the shoulders. So, if you are too tense, it will lead to you pulling too hard. That will end up leading to the shot going over the mark. In addition, it may also lead to sore muscles due to the unnecessary stress on the back and shoulder muscles.

So, the antidote to this mistake is to lay back and relax as much as possible. You can focus your sights on holding the proper form and then releasing. Your follow through will be smooth and effortless. But if you add too much strain on your back and shoulders, you will end up causing more harm than good.

Of course, you don't want to relax too much or else your shoulders will begin to sag. This will lead to the shot falling below the mark. Needless to say, you want to make sure that you have the right form in order to ensure you hit the mark every time.

Mistake number three: not following through

Follow through is crucial in archery. It is part of the execution of the entire shot. That is why your follow through is just as important as lining up the shot, breathing and releasing.

The mistake at this point lies in relaxing ever so slightly at the point of releasing. So, your front hand drops slightly and will cause the arrow to go off mark. When this happens, then you will find that the entire execution was perfect except for the follow through after the release.

The antidote to the mistake is to simply hold your position until after you see the arrow clear the bow. Then, you can exhale and relax. Until then, you need to make sure you hold your mark. Stabilizers can help with this especially under windy, outdoor conditions.

This also plays back to being too tense when holding the shot. If you are too focused on perfect form, you may relax a little bit too early. Then, as the shot is release, the extra movement may cause you to miss the mark.

The fact of the matter is that not following through will cause you to essentially ruin a great set up for your shot. So, a great rule of thumb is to simply take the shot and make sure that you don't exhale and relax until you see the arrow hitting the mark. At that point, you can celebrate a job well done.

Mistake number four: improper release

A proper release is just as important as any other part of your shot. If you release too soon, the draw string will not have generated enough tension. If you release too late (yes, there is such a thing), then you will lose form.

In essence, releasing too late is when you have held a shot for too long to the point where your back hand gets tired of holding the position. This fatigue will lead you to sway or move your fingers needlessly. When this happen, then you will find that the arrow will go off target by a considerable margin.

As such, the ideal perspective on this is to line up the shot, inhale as you draw, hold your shot as your lungs fill with air, count if you must, then release. After your release, you can breathe and relax. In doing this, you will ensure proper form, and proper follow through. The main thing is to avoid putting unnecessary strength into your back hand. Bear in mind that the bow, especially a compound bow, will be set to your particular draw weight. So, you won't have to make any additional effort other than that needed to pull back on the draw string to the right draw length.

So, make sure to focus, but also relax as your hold and then release your shot.

Mistake number five: dwelling on the misses

So, what happens if you miss a shot?

If you are just learning the ropes, it is a part of the process. However, if you are in a big competition, missing a shot can certainly mean the difference between victory and defeat. This is especially true for highly competitive individuals who always want to be the best that they can be. If you happen to find yourself missing a shot, there is not much you can do other than take a deep breath and be ready for the next one.

This is something that happens in all sports. Basketball players miss big shots all the time. Baseball players strike out at the biggest moment of the season. These things happen all the time. Yet, it is common to dwell on the misses a lot more than the victories. If you are unable to move past a mistake that you made or a shot that you missed, then you will have no option but to fail the next time. This is due to the fact that you cannot get past the previous shot.

Even if it sounds too simplistic, it's true: you have to let go of the misses and move on to the next one. The next shot will be better than the last and so on. You cannot expect to miss them all just like you can't expect to make them all.

Please bear in mind that it is your positive mental attitude that will help you become the best archer that you can possibly be. So, don't worry if you miss one shot. You will surely have the chance to make the next one.

Mistake number six: fixing what isn't broken

This is an old cliché, isn't it? After all, why would you fix something that isn't broken?

This is what tends to happen when archers find their groove. Instead of going with what has been working for them, they begin to experiment and tinker around with their mechanics and their rhythm. Of course, archery is a work in progress. So, there is always room for improvement.

However, if you find something that is working for you, then playing around with other types of mechanics may get in the way of your development especially if you are competing. This is why it is best to try out new things when you are not competing or when you are moving from one stage of your development to another.

The last thing that you want to do is to tinker around with your mechanics a couple of days prior to a big competition. Furthermore, messing with your mechanics will only lead to making mistakes when the time comes to compete.

So, if you find yourself on a hot streak, go with it. As you begin to further develop your skills, you can begin to incorporate additional techniques on top of what you know to be working effectively. This will help you to strengthen your personal archery style.

Mistake number seven: cluttered mind

Focus and concentration are the two core tenets of a successful mental state during a shot. However, it is easy to have your mind take over. Often, archers complain that their mind is overrun with thoughts ranging from leaving the stove on to making the rent at the end of the month.

Indeed, it is easy to get caught up in a whirlwind of thoughts. These can only lead to trouble when you are looking to line up your shot and hit the target. Most archers pick happy thoughts such as a family, pets or lovely places.

Other archers visualize the target as a face or an apple. The point is to take your mind away from racing thoughts that will only serve to distract your attention from making what really counts. Ultimately, your ability to make the shot depends on your ability to follow through on all the steps that are needed in order to make a successful though.

In competition, it might be easily to get rattled by the crowd around. And while it is asked of the audience to keep quiet while archers make their shots, that doesn't take away from the distraction that comes with being under the scrutiny of others. So, bear in mind that there are only so many things you can control. You can't really control much more than what is in your hands.

Mistake number eight: Incorrect draw length

We touched upon this point earlier in this guide. We stated how important it was to have the right draw length when choosing the right size of arrows for your particular draw length. Indeed, this is one of the most important points you can consider when making your shots.

However, you may also find that over time, you may end up pulling too much on the draw string. This happens when you begin to gain additional strength. So, the draw weight may become too light for you. At this point, you would need to readjust your draw weight on a compound bow.

In the case of a recurve bow, you might want to check out a different type of bow, or just be aware of how you are over stretching the draw string. The main thing to keep in mind is that you need to have the right length. Otherwise, your shots won't line up properly.

Also, drawing too hard can damage the string. While it will not break the bank to have a draw string replaced, it can lead you to have an unfortunate accident at some point. If you are using a trigger, for example, it could snap before you intend to release and hit you in the face. Naturally, that is a very dangerous accident to have.

So, it pays to take the necessary precautions to make sure that you have the proper form and the right style. That way, your shots can line up correctly time and time again.

Mistake number nine: punching it

Simply put, punching is when you are trying to make a shot happen. You are forcing a shot to happen when you might simply not have the shot lined up. When you begin to punch, you are essentially trying hard to make a shot happen when you simply need to take a step back.

Of course, there are always corrections to be made in order for you to hit the right shot.

However, it is a completely different thing when you are forcing yourself to make a shot that might not be there. This is critical when you are considering pressure that comes with a competition.

Imagine that you find yourself competing. You might be tempted to force yourself to make that perfect shot especially if there are windy conditions. Or, you might force yourself to focus on a point that just isn't there.

So, what to do?

In addition to taking a step back, you can focus on making the most of your shot by making the necessary adjustments to your position. So, if you are going for a longer distance, for example, you might want to try a shorter distance. Or, you can just focus on your point, breathe and let your mechanics take over. Most of the time, you will make the shot. But if you are thinking about making the perfect shot, then you will begin punching.

Needless to say, there is no amount of forcing yourself that will lead you to hit the "perfect" shot. There is always some degree of human error which you need to account for. After all, we would have to be robots in order to be perfect all the time.

After considering some of the most common mistakes when using a compound bow, let's consider some of the most common errors when dealing with a recurve bow.

Mistake number one: losing your target

By far, this is the most common issue with recurve bows. Even though professional recurve bows have sights, it is still very easy to quickly lose track of your target. This is due, in part, to holding a shot for too long. When that happens, you will find yourself struggling to get back on the mark.

In such cases, the best thing to do is just to take a step back and regroup. Often, that's all it takes to get back on track and make the right shot. Other times, it is common for archers to begin punching it. Thus, the right shot will never come.

If you are using a sight, you will notice that it is a circle with a line in the middle. So, focusing on the line alone, as opposed to the entire circle, will go a long way toward helping you stay on the mark. The most important thing to bear in mind is that if you "forget" about the circle, it'll just be you and target. The bow and the arrow are just the means toward reaching the target.

Mistake number two: forcing your aim

This is a perfect continuation of the previous point. When you begin to force your aim, you end up trying to focus on a mark that may not be there. If you are using a sight, then you have everything you need in order to line up the shot.

However, if you are not using a sight, then it become even more important to rely on your instincts and your eyesight. Naturally, going without a sight is far more challenging. But also, it is far more tempting to try and make a shot that you are not even sure is there. This is why you need to be focused and concentrated on what you are looking to aim.

At the end of the day, forcing your aim may just be a sign that you are tired and you need a break. In competition, it might be a sign that the pressure is starting to get to you. So, just try to take a break, relax and get ready to release.

Mistake number three: holding on too long

Much like using a compound bow, holding on too long may lead you to force the shot. While you might also be pulling to far on your draw length, holding on too long will cause you to lose your target. This will lead you to miss your shot. So, you might feel compelled to hold on even longer in order to attempt and regain your shot.

Needless to say, when you hold on too long, you are only forcing yourself to make a shot that isn't there anymore. When you are having fun, it is very easy to just regroup. In competition, things change dramatically.

Once technique that some archers like to use is just the standard 3... 2... 1... countdown. You can begin your countdown as soon as you are set at your proper draw length. If you feel that you need less time, then a "1, 2" count will suffice.

Bear in mind that letting go too soon will cause a similar type of effect. So, it is best for you to focus, concentrate and make sure you have the right shot lined up before letting go.

Mistake number four: going against the wind

Isn't this one a classic?

The wind is one of the trickiest factors that archers have to deal with. It not only causes unnecessary movements, but it can also lead you to squint needlessly or even get hair in your face.

So, taking precautions on windy days is crucial in ensuring that you will hit your marks.

If you have long hair, making sure it stays put is critical toward keeping it clear. Also, wearing protective glasses will help you keep dust and dirt from getting in your eyes. After all, could you imagine a gust of wind blowing dirt into your eyes right when you have your shot lined up?

Needless to say, you want to make sure that those precautions are also taken care of.

The use of stabilizers is also recommended on very windy days. The added weight will help you stay balanced and ready to fire when needed.

In competition, it is important to make sure that you understand the applicable rules to your event. There are cases in which recurve competitions may not admit the use of stabilizers. In other cases, you may have to forego a sight. So, it all boils down to the specific circumstances you are in.

Mistake number five: worrying too much on equipment

Do you recall an earlier point we made: equipment will never make up for a lack of training and practice?

Indeed, it is very true. You may have the most expensive equipment out there on the market. Yet, it will only help you get so far. Your training and practice will help you take an ordinary piece of equipment and get fantastic results.

This goes for your bow and your arrows. There are no magic arrows that will always hit the center of the bull's eye despite having improper form. The best shooters in the world are all about developing technique when can be repeated over and over again. They are keen on finding the right stride and then replicating it until it becomes second nature to the them. Just like golfers, clubs are meaningless if they don't have the right swing. The same goes for archers. Unless you have some enchanted bow, your success will boil down to your individual ability and skills. So, it certainly pays to be focused on developing as much as you can and let the equipment take care of itself.

Mistake number six: losing form

The core tenet or recurve shooting is your back tension. Maintaining your back and shoulders aligned are critical to developing a good shot. So, you cannot expect to hit the mark if your back suddenly goes soft or if you hunch over.

By the same token, you cannot expect to stand up too straight and rigid, as if you were a robot.

That will only cause you to have stiff movements which will hinder your ability to hit the mark. So, taking deep breaths as you ease into position is critical in order for you to sustain the proper form. Once you do that, then you will be able to hit your mark every time.

Also, make sure that you stretch before each round of shooting. When you do that, you will be able to feel lose and ready. If you are feeling sore or have some kind of muscle pain, then you might consider taking a mild painkiller just to help you get loose.

In the case of children, if they are feeling stiff or just plain sore, then letting them play around for a few minutes usually helps them loosen up. Remember that this should be a game especially in the case of children. So, giving them the opportunity to have fun is essential to helping them develop proper form.

Mistake number seven: you forget to push

Wait a minute, push?

Yes, that's right. With your back hand, you pull on the draw string. With your front hand, you push on the bow. This will allow you to find the right tension you need. This will enable you to avoid putting too much strain on one hand. What this implies is that if you don't push with your bow hand, then your front hand will become too stiff from the strain of holding the bow. This will also cause you to pull too hard with your draw hand. Needless to say, you will not have the proper form.

In a way, you should think about your position as if you were "opening" the bow. That can help you to use both hands for the same purpose. In the end, you will not only hold your position perfectly, but you will also be able to ease the strain on your back and shoulders.

By holding your position properly, you will also reduce the likelihood of injury. So, it is certainly a very important aspect to keep in mind as you begin to develop your own, individual form. Please keep that in mind: your form is yours and your only. It is similar to a baseball pitcher's mechanics. The fundamentals are the same, but in the end, the mechanics of the wind up and delivery are unique to each pitcher. So, always strive to develop the style that works for you.

Mistake number eight: panic!

Imagine you have everything lined up. You have the right shot and you have your mark.

Suddenly, your mind goes blank and you have a small moment of hesitation. It happens; and it happens when you overthink things. You might be overthinking your form or your aiming. You want everything to be lined up just so. Then, when the time comes to take the shot, you have a split second of panic in which you doubt your form and technique.

At this point, you have two choices: you either let go of the shot and let your form do its job, or you step back. In competition, the latter may not be an option. In the regular world you can always step back, compose yourself, and then line up your shot again.

The most important thing to keep in mind that your mechanics will dictate your success. You cannot expect to do more than your training has afforded you. If there is perfect out there, then someone may reach it one day. Until then, perfection is not within the human realm of possibility. This means that we are vulnerable to mistakes.

We are also vulnerable to feeling insecure at times. So, all you have to do is take care of those aspects which you know you can control and let the rest take care of itself. After all, we are not yet able to control the wind. As such, you might as well let the wind take care of itself while you take care of your shot. At the end of the day, that's what counts and nothing else.

Mistake number nine: trying to be perfect

Speaking of perfection, you can never expect to be perfect.

What does that mean?

It means that attempting to be perfect will only lead you to overthink things. You will become obsessed with trying to achieve a standard that may not even be there.

The best you can strive for each day is to improve upon yourself and your performance. This will help you make the most of your training and your ability to develop your skills to a whole new level each time. By ensuring that you try your best on a consistent basis, you will be able to achieve your personal style. Your personal style will make you into the best archer you can possibly be.

It is also vital for you to avoid comparing yourself to others. Sure, there are those you are better than you, but that is not because they are more talented than you are. It is simply the result of their hard work and dedication. With time, you too will be able to develop and hone your skills to an equal level as those around you.

So, strive each day to outperform yourself. That is the only thing which you can really control. Everything else may very well be beyond your control. In competition, all you can do is your best. You cannot control what everyone else does. Ultimately, your performance and your outcomes will be dictated by what you put into it and nothing else.

So, there you have it. We have discussed 18 points which can very well adapt themselves to virtually any situation in archery. Please take the time to meditate upon these points. At the end of the day, you will find that being the best you can be is the only real goal to keep in mind.

Chapter 6: Becoming a successful archer

In this chapter, we are going to take a look at some more general guidelines which you can follow in order to become the best possible archer you can become.

It should be noted that archery is just like any other sport out there: it requires effort and dedication in order for you to become as good as you possibly can.

Over the last couple of chapters, we have focused on the actual mechanics of archery. Yet, there is a lot more to archery than just getting cool equipment and making great shots. Archery requires a holistic mindset that will lead you to achieve a sustainable system. This system should allow you to make shot after shot especially if you are competing.

Archery, as we have established before, is like any other sport in the sense that you must develop your own personal style. So, when you consider the mechanics behind developing your own style, you need to see which elements work right for you and which do not.

One of the best ways of finding out what works and what doesn't is by asking around. Other archers can provide you with their own personal insights. This can help you to experiment with those elements which help you feel comfortable.

The other main component to developing proper mechanics and style is your ability to focus and concentrate. Indeed, archery is not for those individuals who need to be in constant motion. If you are one of those people who need to run around all the time, then you might consider going for a run before hitting the archery range.

Archery is similar to golf in the fact that it does not have explosive movements, but it does have very calculated and precise motions. When you think of golf, you think about the finesse it takes to sink a putt. Archery works very much the same way. You cannot expect to hit very precise shots without finding a sweet spot that will enable you to calculate your movements with surgical precision.

So, we will be discussing some of the most important points which you must consider when taking up archery. These go beyond the actual practice of the sport and focus more on the personal aspects which you can put into practice when picking up a bow.

These relate to nutritional and physical aspects, as well as, psychological factors. In particular, your mindset is essential in helping you become successful at this sport.

Let's take a look the key factors which you can use to get the most out of your archery endeavors.

Factor number one: nutrition and conditioning

As with any sport, nutrition plays an important factor in developing healthy habits and achieving ideal physical conditioning. In the particular case of archery, you won't find outrageous nutritional demands such as those seen in swimmers and track athletes.

The fact of the matter is that anyone who takes up archery should strive stay in the best possible physical condition. This will enable you to handle the rigors of competition. If you do not choose to compete, then good condition is essential in order to ensure that you will be able to enjoy the sport without having any physical limitations that might keep you from actually carry out any of the tasks related to the sport.

For starters, you need to be able to support the weight of the bow. Since bows are much lighter today than they used to be in the past, you won't expect to carry a huge amount of weight with one hand. Nevertheless, you should expect to be able to hold up the bow for a few minutes at a time while you line up your shot and then release.

That may not seem like a lot of stress on your arms, but after a couple of hours' worth of practice, you might begin to feel the burn. The same goes for your draw hand. You need to be strong enough to pull on the draw string in order to make the shot.

Of course, you have the option to adjust the draw weight on the bow if you are using a compound bow. But still, you need to have at least some type of physical strength in your arms in order to carry out the maneuvers with proper form and mechanics.

Most archers keep physically fit by having a balanced nutrition and having a regular exercise routine. The main focus of archers is upper body strength though having strong core muscles (lower back and abdomen) are crucial in order to maintain proper form therefore the course of several shots.

Also, having strong legs is important as your legs are vital in keeping you upright. In addition, you will have to stand for extended periods of time. So, having strong legs is a good way to help keep your posture strong and not become overly fatigued when you are called upon to shoot.

Competitive archery will place greater demands on your body especially if you have to travel around to take part if various circuits or events. So, getting enough sleep and rest is fundamental in order to make sure that you feel physically able to carry out the activities related to a competition.

Yet, there is one very important reason why sleep and proper rest are essential to being a successful archer: you need to maintain focus and concentration especially during a competition. So, needless to say, if you are sleepy, you won't be able to focus properly. This will lead to through any number of complications when looking to make your shots.

Also, if you take any type of medication, it is important that you understand if it makes your drowsy or dizzy. If it does, then you might not be able to focus quite as well as you would like to. So, you might have to play around with your dosage in order to make sure it doesn't affect you especially during a competition. If that is the case, then it is recommended that you check with your doctor first.

Then, there is the topic of hydration. It is vital to keep proper hydration as a loss of minerals and electrolytes can lead your chemical levels to become unbalanced. Aside from the uncomfortable physical symptoms of dealing with unbalanced electrolyte levels, you will not be able to focus properly.

As you can see, the main point behind these tips is to help you stay clearheaded especially during a competition. As such, you need to be just as fit mentally as you do physically in order to stay on top of your game.

Factor number two: mental concentration and focus

We have discussed mental concentration and focus quite a bit throughout this guide. Concentration and focus are essential to making the right shots especially in competition.

At first, achieving full concentration may be next to impossible. When you are first attempting to find your groove and your personal style, you might be overly conscious about your movements and your mechanics. As such, you may not be able to fully concentrate on the shot itself as opposed to actually making it.

This is why brand-new archers tend to fire without really concerning themselves about hitting specific targets. Rather, their focus is more on developing the proper mechanics which then makes it easier to hit any shot.

Naturally, everyone wants to hit targets right from the beginning. However, doing so may be very difficult without learning the proper mechanics and style. That being said, proper form can be ruined by an improper mindset.

Think about it this way: your body is doing all the right things, but your mind is not in the right place. What this does is lead your mechanics astray. That, in turn, will keep you from hitting your shots.

So, what can you do about it?

Developing mental focus and concentration can be achieved through any number of ways. The most important way in which you can ensure you have that focus is to be certain about your mechanics. If something doesn't feel right, or if anything feels off, then chances are it will mess around with your mind.

If you have ever heard sportscasters talk about how players can't seem to get comfortable, that is exactly what they mean.

Professional athletes know when something isn't right. They can sense it when they are not at the top of their physical condition. As such, they tend to feel off. You can tell when top athletes are playing hurt.

The same can happen to you if you are not feeling right physically. So, if you are not doing well, for whatever reason, then you must consider taking some time off. If you are in the middle of a competition, you might consider withdrawing. There is only so much you can do to "power through".

Do you recall the earlier point about "punching"?

When you start to force shots then you ultimately end up missing them because the shot just isn't there. This might be due to a sore back or tight shoulders. It might also have to do with a bad shot that just, somehow mess with your mechanics.

Consequently, you might just have to take a step back and regroup. If you are dealing with injuries, you might consider getting them checked out in order to avoid bigger issues. Sometimes all you have to do is take some time off and recover. Any professional athlete will tell you that playing through nagging injuries is never easy and may only aggravate the problem down the road.

When you are dealing with psychological issues, for instance, you just simply had a bad day, that too can get to you. Often, the pressure of competition can also build up lead you to lose focus.

Developing mental focus is easier for some than it is for others. For some archers, mental focus can be achieved through mantras.

A mantra is just a phrase that you repeat to yourself over and over. You may even see some moving their lips as they line up their shots. The purpose of a mantra is to take your mind off everything else and let you focus your sights on the target.

You can use anything you want as a mantra so long as it makes sense for you. This could be a catch phrase or a motivational quote. It could just be a single word. Whatever it is, it just something to help take the tension away from what is really going on at the moment.

Other archers find that visualization helps. Earlier we mentioned visualizing the target as a face or a fruit, like an apple. Other types of visualization might be seeing the target for what it is: a target. So, you know that if you make that shot, you will be "making it". It is just another step on your way to become the best archer that you can become.

This last point is very important. You cannot expect to make the next shot. You can only make the shot that is in front of you. It is impossible to make the next shot because it isn't there yet.

When you focus on making the shot in front of you, you will become clear in the fact that you can only control what is in your hands. Understanding this is a great way of relieving stress and anxiety. This is very important to keep in mind especially in competition.

In competition, you cannot control what the other competitors do. If only you could control the shots they make and don't make. But the reality is that you cannot control a single thing anyone else does. The only thing you can control is what you do. So, it is best to keep any other ideas out of your head. The better you are at keeping other ideas out of your mind, the easier it will be for you to make you own. The rest will take care of itself.

Factor number three: practice

There is a lot of questions surrounding the right amount of practice that you should get.

Indeed, there is no right answer to that question.

The fact of the matter is that the right amount of practice is a relative thing. You see, practice depends on a number of factors such as your overall lifestyle and the amount of time you can dedicate to archery. Also, it depends on what purpose you have for archery.

Is it just a hobby for you?

Is it just another pastime?

Or, are you serious about competing and earning a few tournament wins?

Answering these questions will determine how much practice you need to get in order to achieve the skills that you need to achieve in order to become the best possible archer that you can be.

For starters, let's assume that you are taking up archery as a new pastime. So, you are keen on developing your skills though you might not be too intent on turning professional. So, you can schedule your practice sessions to fit your schedule. In a way, you can use archery in much the same way some folks use golf to relieve stress.

Under this premise, you might look at having weekly training sessions. Perhaps you can go out to the range two or even three times a week. In such cases, archery can really help you unwind and relieve stress from your day to day occupations.

If you are more inclined to participating in renaissance fairs and such, you can take up archery as part of a broader pastime and passion. Perhaps you already take part in fairs and reenactments, but you've just now decided to give archery a try. So, you can choose to take some archery lessons just to get you on the right track. Then, you can practice at fairs and events in order to beef up your skills.

Now, if you are serious about become a pro, then you will have to dedicate a great deal of time and energy to developing your skills. This might mean a combination of lessons, training and practice out in the range.

One of the truly incredible things about archery is that there is no age limit to it. Plus, you don't need to have any exceptional physical qualities such as being unusually tall like a basketball player or have unbelievable speed in the case of sprinters.

You can take up archery regardless of your initial physical conditioning, or even lack thereof. However, if you are serious about it, you would need to take up much time as possible to get your skills as far along as possible.

In addition, you will have to make time for meets, competitions and events in which you can compete. This often involves travel, too. Consequently, archery, at a competitive level, becomes a lifestyle. In short, it's like any other sport. The dedication that it takes to achieve a highly competitive level is comparable to any other sport out there.

Then, there's a word to be said about hunters.

Hunters can only really put their skills into practice at certain times of the year, most notably, during gaming season. Since gaming season is hardly year-round, hunters need to keep their skills sharp during the off season. With that in mind, it is important to make time for practice and sharpening skills.

Most hunters like to hit the range as much possible. The range can be a great place to try out and experiment with different techniques and approaches. Unlike competitive archery, hunters don't necessarily need to focus style and form in order to make "perfect" shots.

For hunters, being out in the wild in search of prey is hardly the most conducive environment to form and style. So, hunters need to be able to line up their shots under duress and usually in windy or unpleasant conditions.

Also, hunters may have to fire on the run. This is something that professional archers, much less hobbyists won't have to deal with. So, a hunter needs to be able to act quickly, move fast and fire on the go. Hence, hunters will place a greater deal of emphasis on hitting the mark rather than developing perfect form.

At the end of the day, whatever type of archery you pursue, you will need to develop a training and practice regimen which can help you beef up your skills and keep them up. Naturally, the more work and dedication you put into practice and training, the better your skills will become.

Now, the next question becomes: what is the best place to practice?

To begin with, the range is the best place to start. Archery clubs also provide target and great sports to practice. The best thing about archery clubs is that there is the option to mingle with other archers. This is a great way of making new friends and connections. You can learn from others who can share their experiences with you and give you a few friendly points. More importantly, the sense of community that comes within the archery world definitely makes it the whole experience even better.

For hunters, if you must practice out in the woods, taking safety precautions is essential to ensuring fun and excitement. Wearing bright colored clothing is crucial. Also, making sure that you have communication at all times is also fundamental in making sure that you don't get crossed up. As long as you can keep track or everyone, you will be able to avoid a potentially tragic accident.

Factor number four: tracking performance

Whether you are a hunter, aficionado or the next world champion, tracking performance becomes a big issue for archers over time.

The easiest metric for determining performance is by tracking the number of shots you take and the number of targets you hit. So, if you set out to take 10 shots, then perfect performance would be hitting the 10 marks.

In an ideal world, you would be able to reach a proficiency level in which you would be able to hit your mark every time. This is why beginners need to gradually work their way up. As a novice, you can't expect to hit every mark. In fact, hitting just one early on is an achievement to be proud of.

The next metric that is used to measure performance is distance. As you gain more and more proficiency, you will be able to hit targets from further away. Most training begin at 10 meters and gradually moves farther and farther away.

Now, depending on the type of bow that you use, you will be able to hit targets farther and farther away. For instance, a typical recurve bow can hit targets up to a hundred meters away. While there have been some cases in which professional archers have hit longer distances.

Yet, hitting a hundred meters is quite an accomplishment with a recurve bow.

In the case of compound bows, there are some cases in which professional archers have claimed to hit over 300 meters. There are videos online depicting long shots such as these. However, the world record stands at 283.47 meters set in 2015. Thus, hitting any distance beyond 100 meters is quite an accomplishment for any archer let along anything beyond that.

In the case of hunters, their shots usually range from about 20 to 40 yards. In fact, hunters will try their best to get as close as possible. As a matter of fact, it is virtually impossible to make long-range shots in the woods as trees, branches and leaves get in the way. So, hunters need to get as close to their target as possible.

As such, distance can certainly become one of the best ways in which you can track your overall performance and improvement.

Lastly, one other means of tracking your progress is through your own self-assessment.

You will begin to feel more and more comfortable in your shooting stance and draw. As you feel like you have achieved the right mechanics, you will become more and more satisfied with your performance. You will feel how your body adjusts to the natural patterns and motions of shooting a bow.

Regardless of whether you're shooting a recurve or compound bow, both your body and your mind will begin to wrap around. It may sound a little "Zen", but you end up becoming one with your equipment. When that happens, you will be able to achieve a level of familiarity with shooting that you will be second nature.

So, the best means of gauging your progress will be the way you feel about yourself. At the end of the day, the most important thing is that you enjoy the sport and the feel of doing it. The satisfaction that you will get from doing something you truly enjoy is second to none.

One final thought...

When you start out in the world of archery, you will be tempted to compare yourself to others. Needless to say, this is a huge mistake. Everyone develops at a different pace. While you might be well ahead of others at your stage of development, you might not be as far along as others.

By being aware of the fact that archery is a very personal sport, you will resist the urge to think that there are others who are better than you. The main aim of this entire process is to develop your own style; your own way of doing things. As you develop your own style, you will feel that you become the best possible archer that you can become. Otherwise, you would only be copying the style of others.

Of course, there is nothing wrong with trying to take pointers and tips from others which you feel can benefit you, but at the end of the day, the only thing that matters is what you are able to do with the skills and abilities which you have been able to cultivate over time.

Ideally, achieving your own, personal style will lead you to truly enjoy the sport in such a way that it becomes a way of life for you. That, in itself, is perhaps the biggest benefit that you can derive from taking up archery. After all, why spend so much time, effort and even money on something you don't plan to see through?

Archery, like golf or tennis, is one of those sports that becomes a personal passion. As it grows on you, your skills become an extension of your entire self. Once it truly becomes a passion in your life, you will never be able to let it go.

Chapter 5: Becoming a successful archer

In this chapter, we are going to take a look at some more general guidelines which you can follow in order to become the best possible archer you can become.

It should be noted that archery is just like any other sport out there: it requires effort and dedication in order for you to become as good as you possibly can.

Over the last couple of chapters, we have focused on the actual mechanics of archery. Yet, there is a lot more to archery than just getting cool equipment and making great shots. Archery requires a holistic mindset that will lead you to achieve a sustainable system. This system should allow you to make shot after shot especially if you are competing.

Archery, as we have established before, is like any other sport in the sense that you must develop your own personal style. So, when you consider the mechanics behind developing your own style, you need to see which elements work right for you and which do not.

One of the best ways of finding out what works and what doesn't is by asking around. Other archers can provide you with their own personal insights. This can help you to experiment with those elements which help you feel comfortable.

The other main component to developing proper mechanics and style is your ability to focus and concentrate. Indeed, archery is not for those individuals who need to be in constant motion. If you are one of those people who need to run around all the time, then you might consider going for a run before hitting the archery range.

Archery is similar to golf in the fact that it does not have explosive movements, but it does have very calculated and precise motions. When you think of golf, you think about the finesse it takes to sink a putt. Archery works very much the same way. You cannot expect to hit very precise shots without finding a sweet spot that will enable you to calculate your movements with surgical precision.

So, we will be discussing some of the most important points which you must consider when taking up archery. These go beyond the actual practice of the sport and focus more on the personal aspects which you can put into practice when picking up a bow.

These relate to nutritional and physical aspects, as well as, psychological factors. In particular, your mindset is essential in helping you become successful at this sport.

Let's take a look the key factors which you can use to get the most out of your archery endeavors.

Factor number one: nutrition and conditioning

As with any sport, nutrition plays an important factor in developing healthy habits and achieving ideal physical conditioning. In the particular case of archery, you won't find outrageous nutritional demands such as those seen in swimmers and track athletes.

The fact of the matter is that anyone who takes up archery should strive stay in the best possible physical condition. This will enable you to handle the rigors of competition. If you do not choose to compete, then good condition is essential in order to ensure that you will be able to enjoy the sport without having any physical limitations that might keep you from actually carry out any of the tasks related to the sport.

For starters, you need to be able to support the weight of the bow. Since bows are much lighter today than they used to be in the past, you won't expect to carry a huge amount of weight with one hand. Nevertheless, you should expect to be able to hold up the bow for a few minutes at a time while you line up your shot and then release.

That may not seem like a lot of stress on your arms, but after a couple of hours' worth of practice, you might begin to feel the burn. The same goes for your draw hand. You need to be strong enough to pull on the draw string in order to make the shot.

Of course, you have the option to adjust the draw weight on the bow if you are using a compound bow. But still, you need to have at least some type of physical strength in your arms in order to carry out the maneuvers with proper form and mechanics.

Most archers keep physically fit by having a balanced nutrition and having a regular exercise routine. The main focus of archers is upper body strength though having strong core muscles (lower back and abdomen) are crucial in order to maintain proper form therefore the course of several shots.

Also, having strong legs is important as your legs are vital in keeping you upright. In addition, you will have to stand for extended periods of time. So, having strong legs is a good way to help keep your posture strong and not become overly fatigued when you are called upon to shoot.

Competitive archery will place greater demands on your body especially if you have to travel around to take part if various circuits or events. So, getting enough sleep and rest is fundamental in order to make sure that you feel physically able to carry out the activities related to a competition.

Yet, there is one very important reason why sleep and proper rest are essential to being a successful archer: you need to maintain focus and concentration especially during a competition. So, needless to say, if you are sleepy, you won't be able to focus properly. This will lead to through any number of complications when looking to make your shots.

Also, if you take any type of medication, it is important that you understand if it makes your drowsy or dizzy. If it does, then you might not be able to focus quite as well as you would like to. So, you might have to play around with your dosage in order to make sure it doesn't affect you especially during a competition. If that is the case, then it is recommended that you check with your doctor first.

Then, there is the topic of hydration. It is vital to keep proper hydration as a loss of minerals and electrolytes can lead your chemical levels to become unbalanced. Aside from the uncomfortable physical symptoms of dealing with unbalanced electrolyte levels, you will not be able to focus properly.

As you can see, the main point behind these tips is to help you stay clearheaded especially during a competition. As such, you need to be just as fit mentally as you do physically in order to stay on top of your game.

Factor number two: mental concentration and focus

We have discussed mental concentration and focus quite a bit throughout this guide. Concentration and focus are essential to making the right shots especially in competition.

At first, achieving full concentration may be next to impossible. When you are first attempting to find your groove and your personal style, you might be overly conscious about your movements and your mechanics. As such, you may not be able to fully concentrate on the shot itself as opposed to actually making it.

This is why brand-new archers tend to fire without really concerning themselves about hitting specific targets. Rather, their focus is more on developing the proper mechanics which then makes it easier to hit any shot.

Naturally, everyone wants to hit targets right from the beginning. However, doing so may be very difficult without learning the proper mechanics and style. That being said, proper form can be ruined by an improper mindset.

Think about it this way: your body is doing all the right things, but your mind is not in the right place. What this does is lead your mechanics astray. That, in turn, will keep you from hitting your shots.

So, what can you do about it?

Developing mental focus and concentration can be achieved through any number of ways. The most important way in which you can ensure you have that focus is to be certain about your mechanics. If something doesn't feel right, or if anything feels off, then chances are it will mess around with your mind.

If you have ever heard sportscasters talk about how players can't seem to get comfortable, that is exactly what they mean.

Professional athletes know when something isn't right. They can sense it when they are not at the top of their physical condition. As such, they tend to feel off. You can tell when top athletes are playing hurt.

The same can happen to you if you are not feeling right physically. So, if you are not doing well, for whatever reason, then you must consider taking some time off. If you are in the middle of a competition, you might consider withdrawing. There is only so much you can do to "power through".

Do you recall the earlier point about "punching"?

When you start to force shots then you ultimately end up missing them because the shot just isn't there. This might be due to a sore back or tight shoulders. It might also have to do with a bad shot that just, somehow mess with your mechanics.

Consequently, you might just have to take a step back and regroup. If you are dealing with injuries, you might consider getting them checked out in order to avoid bigger issues. Sometimes all you have to do is take some time off and recover. Any professional athlete will tell you that playing through nagging injuries is never easy and may only aggravate the problem down the road.

When you are dealing with psychological issues, for instance, you just simply had a bad day, that too can get to you. Often, the pressure of competition can also build up lead you to lose focus.

Developing mental focus is easier for some than it is for others. For some archers, mental focus can be achieved through mantras.

A mantra is just a phrase that you repeat to yourself over and over. You may even see some moving their lips as they line up their shots. The purpose of a mantra is to take your mind off everything else and let you focus your sights on the target.

You can use anything you want as a mantra so long as it makes sense for you. This could be a catch phrase or a motivational quote. It cold just be a single word. Whatever it is, it just something to help take the tension away from what is really going on at the moment.

Other archers find that visualization helps. Earlier we mentioned visualizing the target as a face or a fruit, like an apple. Other types of visualization might be seeing the target for what it is: a target. So, you know that if you make that shot, you will be "making it". It is just another step on your way to become the best archer that you can become.

This last point is very important. You cannot expect to make the next shot. You can only make the shot that is in front of you. It is impossible to make the next shot because it isn't there yet.

When you focus on making the shot in front of you, you will become clear in the fact that you can only control what is in your hands. Understanding this is a great way of relieving stress and anxiety. This is very important to keep in mind especially in competition.

In competition, you cannot control what the other competitors do. If only you could control the shots they make and don't make. But the reality is that you cannot control a single thing anyone else does. The only thing you can control is what you do. So, it is best to keep any other ideas out of your head. The better you are at keeping other ideas out of your mind, the easier it will be for you to make you own. The rest will take care of itself.

Factor number three: practice

There is a lot of questions surrounding the right amount of practice that you should get.

Indeed, there is no right answer to that question.

The fact of the matter is that the right amount of practice is a relative thing. You see, practice depends on a number of factors such as your overall lifestyle and the amount of time you can dedicate to archery. Also, it depends on what purpose you have for archery.

Is it just a hobby for you?

Is it just another pastime?

Or, are you serious about competing and earning a few tournament wins?

Answering these questions will determine how much practice you need to get in order to achieve the skills that you need to achieve in order to become the best possible archer that you can be.

For starters, let's assume that you are taking up archery as a new pastime. So, you are keen on developing your skills though you might not be too intent on turning professional. So, you can schedule your practice sessions to fit your schedule. In a way, you can use archery in much the same way some folks use golf to relieve stress.

Under this premise, you might look at having weekly training sessions. Perhaps you can go out to the range two or even three times a week. In such cases, archery can really help you unwind and relieve stress from your day to day occupations.

If you are more inclined to participating in renaissance fairs and such, you can take up archery as part of a broader pastime and passion. Perhaps you already take part in fairs and reenactments, but you've just now decided to give archery a try. So, you can choose to take some archery lessons just to get you on the right track. Then, you can practice at fairs and events in order to beef up your skills.

Now, if you are serious about become a pro, then you will have to dedicate a great deal of time and energy to developing your skills. This might mean a combination of lessons, training and practice out in the range.

One of the truly incredible things about archery is that there is no age limit to it. Plus, you don't need to have any exceptional physical qualities such as being unusually tall like a basketball player or have unbelievable speed in the case of sprinters.

You can take up archery regardless of your initial physical conditioning, or even lack thereof. However, if you are serious about it, you would need to take up much time as possible to get your skills as far along as possible.

In addition, you will have to make time for meets, competitions and events in which you can compete. This often involves travel, too. Consequently, archery, at a competitive level, becomes a lifestyle. In short, it's like any other sport. The dedication that it takes to achieve a highly competitive level is comparable to any other sport out there.

Then, there's a word to be said about hunters.

Hunters can only really put their skills into practice at certain times of the year, most notably, during gaming season. Since gaming season is hardly year-round, hunters need to keep their skills sharp during the off season. With that in mind, it is important to make time for practice and sharpening skills.

Most hunters like to hit the range as much possible. The range can be a great place to try out and experiment with different techniques and approaches. Unlike competitive archery, hunters don't necessarily need to focus style and form in order to make "perfect" shots.

For hunters, being out in the wild in search of prey is hardly the most conducive environment to form and style. So, hunters need to be able to line up their shots under duress and usually in windy or unpleasant conditions.

Also, hunters may have to fire on the run. This is something that professional archers, much less hobbyists won't have to deal with. So, a hunter needs to be able to act quickly, move fast and fire on the go. Hence, hunters will place a greater deal of emphasis on hitting the mark rather than developing perfect form.

At the end of the day, whatever type of archery you pursue, you will need to develop a training and practice regimen which can help you beef up your skills and keep them up. Naturally, the more work and dedication you put into practice and training, the better your skills will become.

Now, the next question becomes: what is the best place to practice?

To begin with, the range is the best place to start. Archery clubs also provide target and great sports to practice. The best thing about archery clubs is that there is the option to mingle with other archers. This is a great way of making new friends and connections. You can learn from others who can share their experiences with you and give you a few friendly points. More importantly, the sense of community that comes within the archery world definitely makes it the whole experience even better.

For hunters, if you must practice out in the woods, taking safety precautions is essential to ensuring fun and excitement. Wearing bright colored clothing is crucial. Also, making sure that you have communication at all times is also fundamental in making sure that you don't get crossed up. As long as you can keep track or everyone, you will be able to avoid a potentially tragic accident.

Factor number four: tracking performance

Whether you are a hunter, aficionado or the next world champion, tracking performance becomes a big issue for archers over time.

The easiest metric for determining performance is by tracking the number of shots you take and the number of targets you hit. So, if you set out to take 10 shots, then perfect performance would be hitting the 10 marks.

In an ideal world, you would be able to reach a proficiency level in which you would be able to hit your mark every time. This is why beginners need to gradually work their way up. As a novice, you can't expect to hit every mark. In fact, hitting just one early on is an achievement to be proud of.

The next metric that is used to measure performance is distance. As you gain more and more proficiency, you will be able to hit targets from further away. Most training begin at 10 meters and gradually moves farther and farther away.

Now, depending on the type of bow that you use, you will be able to hit targets farther and farther away. For instance, a typical recurve bow can hit targets up to a hundred meters away. While there have been some cases in which professional archers have hit longer distances.

Yet, hitting a hundred meters is quite an accomplishment with a recurve bow.

In the case of compound bows, there are some cases in which professional archers have claimed to hit over 300 meters. There are videos online depicting long shots such as these. However, the world record stands at 283.47 meters set in 2015. Thus, hitting any distance beyond 100 meters is quite an accomplishment for any archer let along anything beyond that.

In the case of hunters, their shots usually range from about 20 to 40 yards. In fact, hunters will try their best to get as close as possible. As a matter of fact, it is virtually impossible to make long-range shots in the woods as trees, branches and leaves get in the way. So, hunters need to get as close to their target as possible.

As such, distance can certainly become one of the best ways in which you can track your overall performance and improvement.

Lastly, one other means of tracking your progress is through your own self-assessment.

You will begin to feel more and more comfortable in your shooting stance and draw. As you feel like you have achieved the right mechanics, you will become more and more satisfied with your performance. You will feel how your body adjusts to the natural patterns and motions of shooting a bow.

Regardless of whether you're shooting a recurve or compound bow, both your body and your mind will begin to wrap around. It may sound a little "Zen", but you end up becoming one with your equipment. When that happens, you will be able to achieve a level of familiarity with shooting that you will be second nature.

So, the best means of gauging your progress will be the way you feel about yourself. At the end of the day, the most important thing is that you enjoy the sport and the feel of doing it. The satisfaction that you will get from doing something you truly enjoy is second to none.

One final thought…

When you start out in the world of archery, you will be tempted to compare yourself to others. Needless to say, this is a huge mistake. Everyone develops at a different pace. While you might be well ahead of others at your stage of development, you might not be as far along as others.

By being aware of the fact that archery is a very personal sport, you will resist the urge to think that there are others who are better than you. The main aim of this entire process is to develop your own style; your own way of doing things. As you develop your own style, you will feel that you become the best possible archer that you can become. Otherwise, you would only be copying the style of others.

Of course, there is nothing wrong with trying to take pointers and tips from others which you feel can benefit you, but at the end of the day, the only thing that matters is what you are able to do with the skills and abilities which you have been able to cultivate over time.

Ideally, achieving your own, personal style will lead you to truly enjoy the sport in such a way that it becomes a way of life for you. That, in itself, is perhaps the biggest benefit that you can derive from taking up archery.

Chapter 6: Tournament competition

In this chapter, we are going to take a look at the fundamentals of tournament competition. We will be going over the various competition types and tournament formats that are common to archery.

Given that there are various archery tournament formats, we will cover the most common types. Of course, you could basically organize any type of tournament or competition you like. Nevertheless, there are very common types which are played across cities all over the world.

Some tournaments are sanctioned by some official organizing body, some are not. For instance, archery tournaments organized by renaissance organizations generally pit archer versus archer in which the one who hits the most targets is the winner.

Of course, more structured and organized events require a greater detail of planning. So, it certainly helps to understand their formats and how you can take part in them.

First off, we are going to discuss exactly which type of tournaments are available to you. As far as tournaments go, there are three main types of archery: Target archery, field archery and 3D archery, respectively. We are not going to include hunting and traditional archery as they don't generally offer organized or sanctioned tournaments.

In fact, hunting tournaments are generally organized by local groups of hunters. These tend to be held by associations and don't have any specific merit to them in terms of awards or official recognition.

Main guidelines for tournament competition

So, let's take a look at each one, and see how each of these tournaments work based on the type of tournament in question.

Target Archery

Probably the most well-known and popularized type of archery is target archery. Target archery is what you're looking at when you watch Olympic archery on TV. In fact, it's the only type of archery that's shot in the Olympics.

Figure 10. A typical archery target

Types of bows used in target archery tournaments

In target archery archers shoot mainly recurve bows and compound bows. However, only recurve bows are used in Olympic archery. In some instances, other types of bows may be used – but for the most part target archery is down to recurve bow and compound bows.

You will find that there are various categories within Olympic competition, but they all include the recurve bow. The compound bow is not utilized since it is not considered to be a traditional bow under Olympic rules. Although, compound bows are used for international world cup competition.

The good news for newer archers is that only a few tournaments have any stipulations as to who can enter. So, in most cases, you can enter almost any tournament you like.

Plus, most of these tournaments are also pretty laid back, so you shouldn't feel intimidated or too much pressure when you compete. Many of these also actively encourage newer, less experienced archers to enter.

If you're not sure whether or not you're good enough to enter your first tournament yet, just answer the following question: do you hit your targets most of the time?

If your arrows are consistently landing on the target, not the bullseye, just the target itself – it's time for you to enter your first tournament. While you may not win the tournament the first time you enter, you will at least gain valuable experience. Such experience is incredibly useful in your development process. So, it would certainly help to take advantage of the opportunity to gain exposure to a more formal, higher-level shooting experience.

If you're not sure what tournaments are in your area or available for you to shoot in, there are a few ways you can find out. A quick search online for something like: "archery tournament your city, your state" should turn up some good information.

Alternatively, you can always hit your local archery shop, if there's one in your area. They'll be the ones who'll know about all of the local tournaments, as well as other tournaments and events in surrounding states.

Also, if you have an archery club nearby – ask around there too. Even if you're not a member of the club, most archery club members tend to be pretty laid back and helpful to beginner archers looking to get into the sport.

Target archery tournament format

In target archery, there are both indoor and outdoor tournaments. Naturally, the outdoor tournaments are shot during the warmer months of the year. During the winter months, the tournaments move indoors, and the distances shot may vary substantially from the outdoor tournaments. Needless to say, outdoor tournaments will have far longer distances than indoor ones.

Generally, you'll be shooting at targets that are placed around twenty yards from each archer. In outdoor tournaments, however, you'll be shooting at targets at several different distances away. Some tournaments may have "longest shot" contest. So, archers will be challenged to fire from as far away as possible in order to qualify. Usually, the longest, accurate shot will be the winner.

In target archery, outdoor tournaments will feature distances from thirty to ninety meters for men and thirty to seventy meters for women. While indoor target distances tend to be either eighteen or twenty-five meters away from the archer. Again, it all depends on the venue and the conditions. There are outdoor tournaments, such as those at renaissance fairs which only hold target ten meters away. The winners move on based on the number of targets they are able to hit.

In both indoor and outdoor target archery, tournaments are split up into rounds. These "rounds" will be called by different names, depending on where you're competing. They could have different names if you're in the United States, the United Kingdom or Australia. You can check the web site of the organization that runs any tournament that you're thinking of competing in if you want to find out for sure.

In target archery, the organization that oversees all of the tournaments, rules and regulations is the World Archery Federation or WAF. The WAF also oversees Olympic target archery rules as well. So, if you are thinking about pursuing Olympic aspirations, it would be a good idea to become familiar with the rules and formats of the WAF so that you know exactly what to look for.

Many competitions are split up into what are called "ends". In each end, every archer will shoot either three or six arrows. Exactly how many will vary from competition to competition. Again, it is all up to the guidelines of the competition itself, the organizers and the sanctioning body. WAF-sanctioned tournaments usually count toward Olympic qualifying. So, it is certainly worth taking that into account.

Then all of the competing archers will head to the targets to score their shots. Typically, an indoor target archery competition will last for twenty total ends with three arrows shot in each one. This would amount to a total of about 50 to 60 arrows. Almost always, the archer who hits the most targets is the winner. Points are allotted according to the position of the shots. So, a bull's eye is worth the maximum amount of points. It is a similar concept to firearm competitions that have a scoring system for the location of hits on the silhouette.

There is a time limit in these competitions, and all of the competitors will shoot until the end is over. Archers will then shoot at the next target distance, shooting at all of the various distances until the competition is done. There's usually a break for a few minutes about half way into each tournament.

Tournaments are generally a one-day affair that start off early in the morning and finish into the evening. So, it is certainly a great family event if you choose to spend an entire day at an event. Most archers only drink water and have light food during the competition. Naturally, a big, sit-down lunch is not the best way to go during your competition day. So, fruit and a sandwich will be more than enough to get you through your tournament day.

Mind the whistle

Whistles are used to signal the archers for safety reasons. So, it's very important that you pay attention to any whistles you hear and know what the whistle codes mean. This is the most common means of communicating as it is not always easy to yell out instructions or use something like a bullhorn. So, whistles are the instrument of choice for judges and organizers.

Two whistles tells all competitors to step up to the shooting line. A single whistle lets the archers know that they can start shooting. You are not permitted to move beyond the shooting line until all competitors have finished shooting. This means that if you finish first, you must put your bow down and wait for the rest to finish their shots. Then, all shooters move away at the same time. This is done for safety reasons as having people moving around while shots are being fired is a safety concern.

Once you hear three whistles you can approach the target and retrieve your arrows. If you're ever in a position where you feel out of place or you're not sure what to do – just have a look at what the other archers are doing. It could help a beginner from committing a tournament faux pas.

As a last resort, move away from the shooting line and ask for help. If you are not sure what to do, the last thing you want to do is approach the targets. Again, safety is a big concern. So, making and effort to ensure everyone is safe and sound is priority one.

Length of target archery tournaments

For the most part, target archery tournaments tend to take about three or four hours to complete, but they can sometimes go on even longer. As a general rule, plan on spending the day at any tournament you enter, just to be on the safe side.

As indicated earlier, a tournament could start early in the morning and finish into the evening. It really depends on the number of archers especially if it is an open tournament where anyone can enter. So, if there is a higher number of shooters, than each round will take a lot longer to complete. While there will be some drop out due to any number of reasons, it's safe to say that everyone will try their best to complete every round.

Target archery tournament scoring

The circle within a circle type of target used in target archery is scored quite simply. The scores run from ten down to one, with the scores getting lower the further away from the center of the target you hit. Each different colored section away from the bull's eye your arrow hits, the score gets lower.

The "bull's eye" is worth ten points and is mainly referred to as the X ring, as there's a little X on it if you look closely. It's also used for tie breakers – whoever shoots closest to the X wins.

The only difference is in tournaments or competitions using AGB rules. In AGB rules, the different scoring areas are worth nine, seven, five, three and one, respectively.

Competitors will score each end of the tournament by adding up the total score of all of their shots through the entire competition, and the winners are announced.

As such, it is safe to say that you ill get the most points if you make the highest number of shots on the bull's eye. Although, as long as you hit the target, regardless of where, you will still get points. So, unless you miss the target completely on every single shot, you can't expect to be shutout completely. This is why it is so important to hit the bull's eye as much as possible each time you shoot.

Field archery tournaments

In field archery, tournaments can also be shot indoors and out. One of the differences, however, is that while you may be shooting in a straight line – you will also be shooting at targets that are uphill, downhill and other positions. The intent is to replicate real-life conditions as much as possible. So, don't be surprised if there are even obstacles like tree branches and such.

The added challenge of shooting at various distances, angles and target that may be partially obscured is part of what makes field archery so interesting. The targets may or may not have marked distances – meaning you may have to judge the yardage yourself. The extra skill and talent it takes to shoot field archery is sometimes called fieldcraft.

As such, if you find this type of tournament interesting, you will need to go out and practice in the woods. Or, at the very least, attempt to replicate conditions that will be similar to what you can expect at these types of tournaments.

Normally, outdoor field archery is shot in small groups of archers, each taking turns shooting. You will walk a course outdoors, stopping to shoot at each target along the course. These types of tournaments are not always open to the general public. So, you might be asked to have some type of affiliation to a club in order to join. Nevertheless, there are plenty of open tournaments around the county.

In field archery you'll be shooting at one of three different types of targets, depending on which type of "rounds" you're shooting. There are hunter rounds, field rounds and animal rounds, each with their own unique targets and scoring.

Generally, there aren't any moving targets though you might find some tournaments that experiment with these. They use mechanical targets similar to those in field shooting contests that use shotguns and rifles. Again, they are not very common but have become somewhat popular in recent years as a means of mixing things up somewhat.

Figure 11. A field archery competition using a longbow.

Bows used in field archery

In field archery, archers may shoot recurve bows, compound bows and longbows.

Throughout this guide, we have discussed very little about longbows, but they are still used by traditionalists who feel that they add another layer of competition to a tournament. Naturally, these are modern-made longbows that follow specifications of medieval longbows.

There are two main divisions or competition classes in field archery: Individual and team class. There are some other classes that aren't as frequently shot and are a bit beyond the scope of this guide.

Field archery individual tournaments

In individual competition tournaments archers will shoot forty-eight targets over the course of two days. The first day they'll shoot twenty-four targets at various marked distances, while on the second day they'll be shooting at targets of unknown distances. The idea is to measure accuracy both when the distance is unknown and when the distance is unknown.

Both recurve and compound bow archers will shoot three arrows at each target, with their shooting line being marked by red stakes. Longbow archers will shoot the same three arrows per target, shooting from behind blue stakes, which are closer to the targets to compensate for the reduced shooting power of longbows compared to recurves or compound bows.

The archers are scored on the total of all of their shots for the entire forty-eight target tournament. The top sixteen will then move on to the first of the elimination rounds, in which they'll three arrows per archer at twelve targets with marked distances.

Once the first elimination round is scored, the top eight archers will then progress to the second elimination round. In the second elimination round the remaining archers will shoot three arrows at eight targets with marked distances.

Once that round is scored, the top four archers will continue to the semifinals, where they'll compete for the bronze and gold medals. Any ties are resolved with a shoot off – where whoever shoots closer to the X ring wins.

As such, this type of tournament is an elimination tournament as opposed to target archery where no one is eliminated, and points are simply tallied at the end of all rounds.

Field archery team tournaments

In team tournaments, men and women are split into their own divisions. After which, three archers of each bow style are put together into teams. So, there are teams of three that consist of one recurve archer, one compound archer and one longbow archer.

All of the archers shoot in head to head elimination rounds, similar to individual tournaments. In these tournaments, the competition starts at the quarterfinal stage.

The best eight teams will shoot three arrows at each target, one from each archer on the team. They start by shooting at eight targets with marked distances.
The top teams will then move on to the semifinals, in which the two losing teams of the semifinal will compete for the bronze medal – while the winning teams compete for the gold medal.

These rounds are made up of four targets with marked distances, any ties will be resolved the same as in individual tournaments, as mentioned above.

The aren't generally mixed team tournaments though target archery tournaments do tend to have mixed team competitions. This could be an interesting alternative for you to consider competing as well.

NFAA Field Tournaments

The National Field Archery Association, or NFAA, have their own tournament rules which can get quite complicated at times and are a bit beyond the scope of this guide. If you're interested, you can check out their website to see their rules.

As with any archery tournament, if you're at all confused as to what's going on, don't be afraid to ask. You may be surprised at how many of your fellow archers would be happy to show you the ropes. This is why we have mentioned that becoming an archer is also become part of a larger community. You will be able to make plenty of new friends.

3D Archery Tournaments

3D archery is a relatively new type of tournament. They are generally held outdoors though there might be some indoor variations if the facilities permit. They have pretty much the same type of rule and conditions as field archery tournaments except that these types of tournaments use decoys, usually in the shape of animals in order to serve as targets.

There are both smaller, more laid-back local tournaments as well as the large tournaments in which the pros compete for bigger prizes. Both can be a lot of fun to shoot. Open tournaments are well, open, for anyone to join. So, both newer archers and seasoned vets can have the opportunity to get to know one another during a real-life situation.

There are lots of smaller local clubs and organizations across the country, but the ASA and the IBO are the two big ones. Most 3D tournaments and shoots base their rules on one or the other. While these tournaments are locally organized, there are generating quite a bit of nationwide appeal.

Tips and strategies for tournament competition

Once you have made up your mind to take part in a tournament regardless of the type, you can then begin to prepare.

Ideally, you would have at least a few weeks to prepare leading up to the tournament. If you are part of an archery club, they can help you prepare leading up to the tournament. If you are training on your own or with a group of friends, then you can go over the tournament guidelines and at least try to set up your own mock tournaments in order to get the feel for what to expect.

For example, if you are looking to compete in a target archery tournament, you can set up a day in which you can fire off 40 or 50 arrows as a simulation of what you might expect in a real tournament. This is important since firing that many arrows can wear you out. So, you will not be quite as sharp after firing a couple of dozen arrows. This will be a great test to your overall skill level.

In the case of field archery tournaments, going out in to the woods and shooting off a few arrows is virtually essential. You cannot expect to gain proficiency if you don't. So, if you live near a wooded area, or at least can drive up, spending some time shooting at various elevations, through obstacles and even setting up targets in the brush or in bushes will certainly help you get that feel.

Field archery clubs will hold practice events from time to time. So, there are great opportunities to get a feel for what you can expect during a real competition. So, it would certainly be worth taking part in such an event. At the end of the day, the experience which you will get from these types of tournaments will help you become a more proficient archer.

As for hunters, do make sure that you check out your association or club's guideline. They can provide you with all the information and regulations you need to follow in order to take part.

Aside from that, here are some things to keep in mind:

- Hydrate as much as possible. A chemical imbalance may lead you to lose focus and concentration.

- Having a hearty breakfast on tournament day will keep you full during most of the day's activities. So, a light snack should be enough to get you through the entire tournament.

- In outdoor competition, make sure you take scheduled bathroom breaks. The last thing you want to have to deal with is the call of nature during your participation.

- Try to relax and concentrate as much as possible. Being overly tense will only lead you to miss shots and put unneeded pressure on yourself.

- Above all, have fun and enjoy the tournament. You are in it for fun. Even if there is prize money at stake, you are an archer because you like it!

Equipment and accessories used in tournament competition

As far as equipment is concerned, tournaments are fairly straightforward.

However, it is best if you check with the specific tournament guidelines. For instance, Olympic archers use recurve bows with nothing more than sights and stabilizers. Anything beyond that is either not used or not allowed in competition.

Also, compound bows are not used in Olympic competition though there are efforts to introduce them at some point in the future.

Beyond that, the types of bows and accessories used in archery competitions are generally up to the organizers of the event. So, do make sure that you check what is allowed and not allowed so that you can prepare with the specific piece of kit that you will be using on tournament day.

Also, it is important to double check the types of arrows you can use. In general, archers will be asked to use the same type of arrow in order to have an apples to apples comparison among archers. Since using different types of materials for arrows can vary speed and distance, there is generally uniformity among the types of arrows used.

Other types of accessories such as braces and finger guards are standard issue and do not generally have any restrictions. As a novice archer engaging in your first tournament, it would certainly be worth wearing these types of guards as shooting for a few hours on end may lead to injury.

Glasses are also a good idea. If you were seeing eye glasses, then by all means were those. Clear, plastic glasses are also a good idea in order to protect your eyes especially in outdoor tournaments. Some archers like to wear sunglasses though these may be restricted by tournament organizers.

You can also look into wearing those yellow glasses which are meant to reduce glare. These are particularly useful is you are in shadows or perhaps shooting later on in the day. For most indoor tournaments you won't need to very much in the way of eye protection. Just regular eye glasses or clear protective glasses should be more than enough.

By now, you should have a good idea of what to expect at any of the types of archery tournaments we have discussed. So, taking the time to prepare will in advance should give you the opportunity to be ready for your first tournament.

So, do take the time to go over the preparations you need to make. Most of all, keep in mind that having fun and enjoying your time during competition.

Chapter 7: About equipment upgrades and maintenance

In this chapter, we are going to deal with the essential matter of equipment maintenance and even upgrades. Since you might not be very familiar with the intricacies of taking care of such equipment, this chapter is intended to help you get a good feel for what you can do in order to ensure that your equipment is in tip-top shape.

Also, this chapter assumes that you have decided to purchase your own piece of kit. If you are renting at first, but then decide to move on to purchasing your own gear, then understanding the needs and requirements of archery equipment is essential.

General guidelines about equipment maintenance

Archery is, at its core, a sport that deals with equipment. It's not like swimming, running, or martial arts, where you're using your body, and your body only. To be an archer, you need tools, and you can't learn the sport without the proper gear. You can't expect to get very far without any type of gear and equipment on which you can learn the tricks of the trade.

And like all endeavors that require tools, you need to keep your equipment in tip-top shape. You can have the bow of your dreams, but unless you take care of it, it's won't be worth much in a year or two. It's actually kind of surprising how quickly a bow—even a well-made bow—can fall into disrepair, and a bow that hasn't been maintained can not only be ineffectual, it can actually be dangerous.

As you can see, it is imperative to take proper care of your bow and kit. Bows are not exactly cheap. So, it is also a manner of protecting your investment and making it last as long as possible It is far easier to take care of a bow than it is to repair it once it breaks down.

As such, we are going to be taking a look at some pointers on how to keep your recurve and/or compound bow in great shape. Please bear in mind that keeping your gear in good shape doesn't have to break the bank especially if you schedule it at certain points throughout the year.

The importance of having finely tuned equipment

Our starting point is here because it's short and sweet: one of the best ways to keep your bow healthy is to tune it correctly. Find your measurements—make sure you know your exact draw length and figure out a draw weight that works for you and adjust it so that it fits you exactly. There are a lot of posts, articles and videos about tuning your bow, but if you're new to archery and want to get started right away, a bow tech at your local sports shop or outfitter can help you, and if there's an archery range near your house, they usually have folks there who can help you as well.

Although, finding a trusted pro whom you can trust is certainly the best way to go. If you are more inclined to taking care of your equipment yourself, then you might have to spend on some lessons in order for a pro to teach you how to take care of your equipment. Nevertheless, many archery clubs take care of their equipment on their own. So, with such clubs, you can learn how to take care of your equipment on your own.

Make a quick inspection of your equipment after every shot

We tend to think of "maintenance" as something you do when you're not shooting, but the truth is, most bow maintenance is done right before and during a practice session. Here some things to do before and during your practice in order to ensure your equipment is functioning properly and you avoid the risk of it become damaged.

Ensure that you riser is safe to use

All parts of a bow are important, but the riser has a central role in your bow's performance. It's the central hub that unites all parts of your bow, and when you've got problems with your riser, they tend to cause problems in other parts of your bow, as well.

Before you draw your first arrows, check the following:

Look at the grip to ensure it's Stable. Make sure that there are no cracks or gaps in the grip, and that it feels secure—many grips are carved out of the riser itself, but some are attached to the riser, and the attachment (be it with glue or other adhesive) can sometimes loosen or wobble.

Check the area where the riser meets the limbs. Look at the area of the riser that attaches to the limbs, both above and below the riser. These parts of the bow experiences incredible pressure at full draw, so give them a quick look to make sure they're attached properly. If you're using a takedown recurve, make sure the limbs are screwed in properly and tightly; if you're using a compound, make sure there's no "wobble" to the bolts, and the limbs are fixed solidly in place. You do NOT want the limbs to wobble in any way; if they're wobbling, take the bow to your nearest bow tech immediately.

Ensure that your accessories are properly installed. The riser is often where the majority of your accessories, namely, your arrow rest, you bow sight, your stabilizer, and if you're using a compound bow, your cable guard and quiver attachment are located, and you'll want to check all those add-ons as well in order to make sure that:

- They're attached tightly. Loose accessories can be ineffective (a loose bow sight is going to be no use when you're aiming) but they can also be dangerous: a wobbly arrow rest can send your arrows flying in all sorts of directions, and that is definitely a bad thing; and

- There are little to no "erosion marks." After repeated use for many months, you may find that certain parts of your bow get worn down. This is most easily seen on your arrow rest if you're using a recurve, but you can also see erosion on a containment rest and/or a whisker biscuit. When you see that a part is worn down, it's usually telling you that it's time to replace that part.

Taking care of the bow string

Of all the bow's parts, the bow string requires the most frequent maintenance because it's the most prone to wear and tear. Although modern bowstrings are made from complex polyethylenes, they still behave like the bowstrings of flax, hemp, and animal sinew that were common long ago, and they fray and snap when overstressed or simply used too much.

Here are a few things to look out for during your archery practice:

Take a really good look at that bow string. It's hard to stress how important this is. If you find frayed threads, or locations on the string where it looks atypical or different from the rest of the string, replace the string (if you're using a recurve bow) or take it to your nearest bow tech to be replaced (if you're using a compound). Shooting a bow with a faulty string is incredibly dangerous, and fixing it is not something you want to put off.

During your review, make sure you check all parts of the string, too—not just the area where you nock your arrow. If you're shooting a recurve, look at the nocking point, the area above and below the nocking point, and the area where the string attaches to the limb (that's the part that curves forward; the reason why recurves are called recurves because they "re"curve forward), and if you're shooting a compound, check the D-loop, the area above and below the D-loop, the string at the cams (and make sure it's aligned and not leaning right or left), but also check the cable, and make sure the cable is securely fastened in the cable guard.

Again, if you find frayed threads, or locations on the string where it looks atypical or different from the rest of the string, replace the string as soon as possible (if you're shooting a recurve) or bring it to your favorite bow tech to be replaced (if you're shooting a compound).

Keep your string in shape with wax. One of the best ways to maintain the integrity of a bow string is to wax it. There's some debate as to how often you should wax your bow string—some of the stricter folks say after every session, but that can be a bit much, and can actually be detrimental to the string—while others say you should wax it every few sessions. That's probably good enough for most folks—once a week should do it.

Listen closely as you release your arrows. If you're bow makes a lot of noise when you shoot it, or if you can feel that it's vibrating a lot, that can mean the bow strings are loose. Give the bow string (and cables, if you're using a compound) a good review to make sure they're tight.

If you're shooting a recurve, use a bow stringer. They may take a little longer than simply using your legs (also known as the "step-through" method), but bow stringers are most definitely a "best practices" way to prevent the bow's limbs from warping and the tips from injuring you as you try to put on the bowstring. We've actually written an entire post about why using a bow stringer is a good idea, so check that out.

Store your bow properly

We imagine that most "wear and tear" happens to bows while we're using them, but how we store bows is important, too.

Here are a few tips to remember:

Make sure your bow and bow string are clean. If you've been in the great outdoors, be sure to remove any dirt or grime from the riser, limbs, bow string, and accessories. You'd be surprised how gunked up a bow can get, even if you didn't run into inclement weather.

Consider a bow case for both storage and transportation. Bow cases usually fall into two categories: soft cases and hard cases. Soft cases are fine. They're usually made of a durable fabric and can be great carrying cases. But if you're doing any real travelling, you may want to consider a hard case. They're usually made from hard plastic (and some high-end ones are incredibly strong), and they'll protect your bow while you bring it from place to place.

If you don't need a case, hang it up someplace. It's easy to toss it into a corner of the shed or garage, but that usually leads to some kind of build-up on the string or the cams (if you've got a compound bow). Try to hang it on a peg up high someplace—you'll keep it clear of grime, and it'll be tougher for pets / nosy neighbors / kids to get to.

Be careful about heat. Heat can be brutal. Not only can it delaminate the bow's limbs, but it can also erode bow strings and cables. So, if you've tossed your bow in your car or truck, be careful about leaving it in there too long, especially if you've got the windows rolled up. Also be careful with storage spaces, like attics—they can get pretty darn hot, and you don't want to drag your bow out, only to find it's undergone some structural damage.

Have an annual inspection done by a recognized expert

Have you ever head a saying that goes, "a stitch in time saves nine?" It means, basically, that preventing damage is easier than fixing it, and that is most definitely the case with bows. In the same way that you'd bring your car or truck to the garage for a once-a-year tune-up, a full, once-a-year review by an experienced bow tech can be a great idea. He or she will review the bow top to bottom, and look for alignment issues, inconsistencies with cam timing, and a couple other dozen things you'd never think to look at. Unless you, yourself, are a professional bowyer, it can't hurt to have someone who works with bows for a living give your rig a look.

Avoid dry firing at all costs

Even if you already know that you shouldn't dry fire a bow, there are a few tips in this section you might not have occurred to you, so we'd urge you to read on.

Most archers know what a "dry fire" is, but we'll define it anyway: "dry firing" is when an archer draws back his or her bow and releases the bow string without an arrow on the bow string. It's a big, big no-no, and it tends to happen in two ways:

- People either don't know about dry firing, or think their bow is somehow special, and dry fire without an arrow. In a way, it's like firing a gun without bullets. Sure, you can do it, but if you continuously do it, you will be affecting the internal mechanism of the gun. The same thing happens to arrows. The pressure that builds up without the corresponding weight of the arrow only provides needless wear on the bow string.

- They nock an arrow, but don't do so properly, and then release the bow string. Needless to say, if you nock an arrow improperly, your shot will not only miss, but it will also make it harder on the bow string. As such, it will suffer from needless wear and may even begin to fray prematurely.

As you can see, dry firing bad for your bow, but it can also be incredibly dangerous to you and the people around you. The string and/or cable can snap and whip your eye out, or parts of the bow can projectile launch and hit you or someone around you, or something even worse. So, if you just look at it in terms of a safety precaution, you should be good to go. Please remember that safety is of the utmost importance. So, making sure that you have the right precautions in place will help you protect yourself and those around. The last thing you want to is to cause an accident which could have been easily prevented.

It's also worth mentioning that you, yourself, may be very careful with your bow, but you also need to be careful when you lend your bow out to other people, in particular, inexperienced archers. Inexperienced archers are the ones most likely to dry fire a bow because they are new to the sport and don't know what they're doing, so be careful when you're showing off your gear.

Again, it is like showing a gun to someone who is unfamiliar with handling a firearm. You should take the necessary precautions to ensure that this person won't be handling a live gun. The likelihood of them letting off a round accidentally is very high. Needless to say, that can kill someone around you.

In this case, it may not be quite so dramatic as killing someone around you, but there could not only be a serious injury, but the chances of damaging the bow are quite high. So, whenever you show off your kit to an experienced individual, just make sure that they don't commit an error and dry fire it on the spot.

If someone should go ahead dry fire your bow, review the riser and limbs and string. Also, make sure that you are very, very careful the next time you use it. Closely inspect the whole rig, but particularly the riser and limbs. When you dry fire a bow, all the kinetic energy that is usually transferred to the arrow during the shot gets redistributed throughout the bow, and it can do tremendous damage to the bow, and loosen cables, cams, limbs, and so on. Give it a top-to-bottom look, and if you want to really be careful, take it to a bow tech, to make sure it's still structurally sound.

Perhaps it might sound a bit overly dramatic, but a bow's structural integrity is essential to making sure it fires correctly once you intend to use. Imagine if you had a gun with a crooked barrel. You think you are shooting in one direction when the shot is actually going in a different one. This is pretty much the same situation.

There are two more tips about dry firing we should mention, before we move on:

- Always shoot arrows that are the right weight and spine. If you have a heavy bow and you shoot arrows that are far too light or far too flexible, your bow may be gobbling up more kinetic energy during a shot than it's supposed to. Always make sure you're using arrows that are heavy enough and stiff enough for your rig.

- Before every shot, make sure your arrow nocks (the cleft-looking thing at the back of the area) is in good shape. This sounds insignificant, but it's actually really important: if you think about it, a lot of the kinetic energy from the bow is transferred to the arrow and transferred to the arrow at the nock. It's got to be very strong to handle all that energy, so looks for chips or cracks, because a nock that falls apart when the bow string pushes against it, is bad news, and that's another way a lot of dry fires occur.

Needless to say, this can cause a serious accident, both to the archer and everyone else around.

Also, there are two other important items to keep in mind.

Be Stingy with Your Bow. We like to eschew a "share and share alike" philosophy, but that may not be the best policy when it comes to bows. The way you shoot your bow can be very unique, and bows can become conditioned to your style of drawing—so anyone other than you who uses the device may damage it.

Kids outgrow bows, and that can be dangerous. This is actually related to the last tip. When young archers grow, their draw styles change and their bows cease to fit their bodies, leading to a need for new equipment. If you're a parent, be careful about falling into the trap of thinking that "one size fits all"—it doesn't, and an improperly tuned bow can be dangerous. Make sure your child is using equipment that fits him or her and keep an eye out for growth spurts. You'll want to review his/her archery equipment to make sure it's still safe.

How to know if upgrades are needed

While there is new equipment coming out all the time, there are significant upgrades over a year or two. In fact, significant upgrades in bow technology tend to happen over longer periods of time. So, thinking that you need to upgrade, much the same way computers and electronics are upgraded really isn't necessary.

In many ways, it's like a car. Cars change significantly over years but not from one model year to the next. What this means is that you need to keep in mind that "upgrading" is a relative term.

For example, if you are shooting a recurve bow and you're think about "upgrading" to a compound bow, keep in mind that one is not different than the other. It is just a different type of bow. By the same token, things like sights, arrows and arrowheads don't necessarily imply that one is better than the other. They are just suited for different situations and circumstances.

So, how to know when you need to upgrade?

This can happen as the result of an inspection. Your pro can tell you that certain parts are worn and are in need of replacing. This would be the ideal time to get the bow serviced and the parts changed so that they fit well and incorporate the new parts.

Beyond that, upgrading does not refer to getting bigger and better piece of equipment. All it means is that you are replacing worn parts with new ones. As long as you take care of your bow, the overall structure should last a very long time. it is the moving parts like cams, and strings which will need eventual replacing.

Another thing to keep is the arrows themselves. Often, arrows get bent and warped over course of their use. Naturally, a bent or warped arrow will not fly through the air as well as a perfectly straight arrow would. While a bent arrow will not make it impossible for you to use it, it might be best suited for practice and not for competition. It will not only cause you to miss your target, but it might end up messing with your mechanics. You might end up altering your delivery and follow through in an attempt to make up for the warped arrow. So, the best way to go is just to get rid of bent arrows when you see them. You can determine this by a simple, visual inspection after every certain number of shots or after your training session. If you happen to miss too many shots in one day, this may be the cause.

Cost considerations

Finally, any discussion on equipment does not

come without considering cost. Of course, any time you invest in a piece of kit, you will have to invest a good sum of money.

A standard bow may very well set you back a couple of hundred Dollars. This would be a standard recurve or compound bow that has all of the basic functionalities. All of the additional bells and whistles are what end up adding to the cost of the equipment.

Under the accessories that you might consider are sights which may range from fifty to a couple of hundred Dollars, bow strings which can cost upwards of a hundred Dollars and stabilizers which may also cost over a hundred Dollars apiece.

On top of that, you have other accessories such as clickers, triggers and so on. It is up to you to decide how much you are looking to spend on such accessories. If you are a hobbyist who is looking to let a few arrows loose, you may not need to spend more than a few hundred Dollars.

However, if you are a serious archer with competitive aspirations, then it would certainly be wise for you to check out some competitions in order for you to get an idea about the type of gear most competitors are using. After all, you cannot expect to figure everything out without actually seeing it in action.

The most important thing to keep in mind is to be incremental. So, you don't want to shell out a big chunk of change for your gear. You want to make sure that you purchase what you actually need. This will help keep your costs down to what you actually need and not what looks cool.

If you are working with a coach, your coach can suggest what things you need in order to continue in your development. You may also experiment with certain things, though experimentation can be dangerous in the sense that you might alter your technique needlessly.

Then, there is the case of children. As mentioned earlier, children tend to outgrow equipment. So, it is best to make sure that you are aware of this. That way, you can plan purchases ahead of time. The last thing you want is to have children use equipment that is not suited for their size.

One final thought: stay away from purchasing used equipment. Unless you have a pro check it out, it will be very dangerous for you to buy used equipment as you may not be sure what kind of a shape it's in. Even if you are getting "a deal", you might end up paying more to get it fixed than what it would have cost new. So, make sure you stay clear of used equipment.

Conclusion

So, there you have it. A complete guide to archery without taking up volumes and volumes. We have discussed the main points of archery, from history to equipment maintenance. You will surely have learned a great deal of information in these pages.

As such, you would have hopefully picked up the most important items that will enable you to get started in the world of archery.

So, what are the next steps?

Well, if you have made up your mind that archery is something you'd like to take up, or something that your children might be interested in giving a try, the next step would be to find out if there are any archery clubs in your vicinity. These clubs can be the best place to begin insofar as actually picking up a bow a firing off a few shots.

Most archery clubs and academies can arrange a demo class so that you can get the feel for a bow and arrow. This is especially important for children. If they feel that this is something they would like to pursue, you will notice them getting excited at their demo lesson. By the same token, if it is something that they would not come to appreciate, then you may find that they will not get very enthusiastic about it.

The main thing is to avoid the temptation of rushing out to buy a bunch of equipment. Doing so may lead you to accumulate a bunch of gear that you may not use ever again. So, at first, renting equipment may be the best way to go. Then, you can ease into purchasing your own gear.

Whether clubs, pros or fellow archers, you can always get advice from others around you. They can give you tips and ideas on brands, materials and sizes of equipment. That way, you can be sure that you know what you are getting. When you are new to the archery scene, it's best to avoid unknown brands or equipment which you cannot get any reliable type of feedback on.

For instance, if you find that some super-duper looking bow is on sale, for a great price, but the brand is completely unknown to you or those around you, then you may be buying at your own peril. So, it is always best to stick to the brands and equipment you know. That way, you can be sure that you are not tossing your money down the drain.

As you begin to get comfortable with archery, you might very well be interested in competing. This is certainly a great way of making your mark (no pun intended) on the archery world. Competing can give you something to look forward to in addition to providing you with a sense of satisfaction and accomplishment. In short, competing is something which you need to consider at least at some point in your archery endeavors.

Of course, it might take some time before you feel comfortable in doing so. However, just the sheer excitement of participating can be a great boost to your training plans.

Also, make sure that your training regimen takes into account a healthy diet, regular exercise and good mental concentration exercises. By combining all of these elements, you can give yourself a good chance at being successful. Naturally, developing skills takes time. Nevertheless, being a successful archer isn't just about taking a bow in your hands and shooting off arrows. It starts with your mindset and then carries over onto the shooting line.

By focusing on a mantra or visualization exercise, you can help reduce the psychological tension that comes with firing off an arrow. Make sure that you feel comfortable when on the line. If you are not comfortable, for whatever reason, then you might want to take a break and breathe. If you are feeling anxious during competition, the last thing you want is to force a shot. Sometimes, all it takes is to lower you bow, take a deep breath and visualize yourself nailing the target.

Please keep in mind that archery should be about having fun and enjoying yourself. Even if you decide to go hardcore and compete at the highest level possible, archery should provide you with the opportunity to make yourself feel "at home" when holding a bow and arrow in your hands.

These are the times when everything else around you dissipates and it is just you and the target. Hence, archery is one of the ultimate sports for folks who are looking to have fun, practice and challenging sport, and combine intellectual with physical skill.

So, thank you for taking the time to read this guide. There are plenty of other articles blogs and books on the subject. By taking the time to read this, you are giving the author a boost of confidence. After all, you are validating a great deal of hard work and dedication that was put into producing this guide.

If you have found this guide to be interesting and information, do make sure to leave a comment so that other interested folks can learn more about how this guide can help them get started with archery and avoid many of the pitfalls that novice archers tend to run into.

Thank you once again and keep in mind that archery is a very personal sport. You own, individual style will evolve as you gain more and more proficiency. You can and will become the best archer that you can possibly be.

Happy shooting!